D0709435

THE INTERNATIONAL
PSYCHO-ANALYTICAL
LIBRARY
NO. 91

THE INTERNATIONAL PSYCHO-ANALYTICAL LIBRARY

EDITED BY M. MASUD R. KHAN

NO. 91

INTRODUCTION TO THE WORK OF MELANIE KLEIN

by
HANNA SEGAL

New, enlarged edition

LONDON
THE HOGARTH PRESS
AND THE INSTITUTE OF PSYCHO-ANALYSIS
1973

Published by
The Hogarth Press Ltd
40 William IV Street
London W.C.2

*

Clarke, Irwin & Co. Ltd
Toronto

ISBN 0 7012 0336 6

Printed in Great Britain by
Butler & Tanner Ltd
Frome and London

CONTENTS

ACKNOWLEDGMENTS

THE BOOK ITSELF is an acknowledgment of the debt I owe to the late Melanie Klein.

I am grateful to my patients for their co-operation in the analytic work, particularly to those who have given me permission to use their material as illustrations in the text.

I am indebted to generations of students at the Institute of Psycho-Analysis in London for the stimulus they have provided in their questions, criticisms and suggestions.

The first edition of this book appeared under the auspices of the Melanie Klein Trust and I received valuable help from the trustees, especially Miss Betty Joseph and Dr. Elliott Jaques.

Mrs. Jean McGibbon compiled the index of the first edition and assisted me with the final version of the manuscript.

I am grateful to my husband for help and support.

H.S.

INTRODUCTION

THIS BOOK is based on a series of lectures given over a number of years at the Institute of Psycho-Analysis in London. As I have been asked repeatedly by students for a transcript of the lecture notes, I concluded that it would be useful to edit them and present them as a book.

The course was designed to introduce the students to Melanie Klein's contributions to psycho-analytical theory and practice. As it was given to students in their third year of psycho-analytical training, a thorough knowledge of Freud is taken for granted throughout. In a limited number of lectures it is possible only to give a rather simplified and schematic description of Melanie Klein's theoretical contributions, but as psycho-analytical theories are derived from clinical experience and meant to throw light on clinical material I rely on my clinical illustrations to convey them more fully.

The lectures are meant as an introduction and not as a substitute for the study of Melanie Klein's own writings. They can be used as a guide to reading. No references are made in the text as they would have to be far too numerous; instead, a list of relevant literature is appended to each chapter.* One exception has been made in the chapter on "The Psychopathology of the Paranoid–Schizoid Position" as Bion's contribution here occupies a unique position, and I have used his own terminology. A full chronological bibliography of Mrs. Klein's works available in English is appended, as well as a selected bibliography of critical writings about her work.

* Only papers dealing with Melanie Klein's work will be listed, as classical analytic literature has been on the curriculum of students in the earlier years of their training.

The order of the chapters is the same as that adopted for the lectures. In a way, the development of psycho-analytical theory is the reverse of the development of the individual. The study of adult neurotics led Freud to discoveries first about childhood and then about infancy, each discovery about the earlier stages of development enriching and illuminating the knowledge of the later ones. Similarly, Melanie Klein, in her work with children, was led to the discovery that both the Oedipus complex and the super-ego are well in evidence at a much earlier age than had been assumed; exploring further, she was led to the early roots of the Oedipus complex, then to her formulations about the depressive position and, lastly, about the paranoid–schizoid position. If one follows the chronological order of Melanie Klein's contributions, the links of her work with that of Freud are much clearer, and one can follow the development of her theories at each stage. On the other hand there are great advantages in beginning with earliest infancy and trying to describe the psychological growth of the individual as we see it now in the light of Melanie Klein's theory. However, starting in that way, one has to begin with those phases of development in which the psychological phenomena are the most remote from adult experience, the most difficult to study, and therefore, not surprisingly, the most controversial. I have decided to try combining both approaches: in the first chapter I give an outline of Melanie Klein's early work, trying to show the development of her work, particularly in the *Psychoanalysis of Children*. I go on to describe the implication of her work for the concept of unconscious phantasy. Then I abandon the historical approach in order to present her definitive views on psychological growth. We have accumulated sufficient knowledge, and our theory is sufficiently comprehensive to warrant an attempt to present it as a whole.

Most of the chapters are devoted to an account of the phenomena in the paranoid–schizoid and the depressive positions, and I think it would be useful, at the outset, to try to elucidate the term "position." In some sense, the paranoid–schizoid position and the depressive position are phases of development. They could be seen as subdivisions of the oral stage, the former occupying the first three to four months and being followed by the latter in the second half of the first year. The paranoid–schizoid position is characterized by the infant's unawareness of "persons," his relationships being to part objects, and by the prevalence of splitting processes and paranoid anxiety. The beginning of the depressive position is marked by the recognition of the mother as a whole person and is characterized by a relationship to whole objects and by a prevalence of integration, ambivalence, depressive anxiety and guilt. But Melanie Klein chose the term "position" to emphasize the fact that the phenomenon she was describing was not simply a passing "stage" or a "phase" such as, for example, the oral phase; her term implies a specific configuration of object relations, anxieties and defences which persist throughout life. The depressive position never fully supersedes the paranoid–schizoid position; the integration achieved is never complete and defences against the depressive conflict bring about regression to paranoid–schizoid phenomena, so that the individual at all times may oscillate between the two. Problems met with in later stages, as, for instance, the Oedipus complex, can be tackled within a paranoid–schizoid or a depressive pattern of relationships, anxiety and defences, and neurotic defences can be evolved by a paranoid–schizoid or a manic-depressive personality. The way in which object relations are integrated in the depressive position remains the basis of the personality structure. What happens in later development is that depressive anxieties are modified and become gradually less severe.

Some paranoid and depressive anxieties always remain active within the personality, but when the ego is sufficiently integrated and has established a relatively secure relationship to reality during the working-through of the depressive position, neurotic mechanisms gradually take over from psychotic ones. Thus, in Melanie Klein's view, infantile neurosis is a defence against underlying paranoid and depressive anxieties, and a way of binding and working them through. As integrative processes initiated in the depressive position continue, anxiety lessens and reparation, sublimation and creativity tend to replace both psychotic and neurotic mechanisms of defence.

CHAPTER ONE

MELANIE KLEIN'S EARLY WORK

ONE COULD DIVIDE Melanie Klein's contributions to psychoanalytical theory and technique broadly into three distinct phases.

The first phase starts with her paper "On the Development of the Child" and culminates in the publication of *The Psycho-Analysis of Children* in 1932. During this phase she laid the foundations of child analysis and traced the Oedipus complex and the super-ego to early developmental roots.

The second phase led to the formulation of the concept of the depressive position and the manic defence mechanisms, described mainly in her paper "A Contribution to the Psychogenesis of the Manic Depressive States" (1934) and "Mourning and its Relation to Manic Depressive States" (1940).

The third phase was concerned with the earliest stage, which she called the paranoid–schizoid position, mainly formulated in her paper "Notes on some Schizoid Mechanisms" (1946) and in her book *Envy and Gratitude* (1957).

There is a significant change in her theoretical outlook, from the time of her formulation of the concept of positions in 1934. Up till that time she followed Freud and Abraham in describing her findings in terms of libidinal stages and the structural theory of the ego, super-ego and id. From 1934 onwards, however, she formulated her findings primarily in terms of her own structural concept of positions. The concept of "position" does not conflict with the concept of the ego, super-ego and id, but it purports to define the actual structure of the super-ego and the ego, and the character of their relationship in terms of the paranoid–schizoid and depressive positions.

I want to devote this chapter to Melanie Klein's work before 1934, to show how it evolved from the classical Freudian theory, at what points it began to differ from it, and how the early ideas foreshadowed the later formulations.

When Melanie Klein started analysing children in the 1920s she threw new light on the early development of the child. As is often the case in scientific development, new discoveries follow the use of a new tool, whilst they in turn can lead to the refinement of the tool. In the case of child analysis the new tool was the play technique. Taking her cue from Freud's (1920) observations of the child's play with the reel, Melanie Klein saw that the child's play could represent symbolically his anxieties and phantasies. Since small children cannot be asked to free-associate, she treated their play in the playroom in the same way as she treated their verbal expressions, i.e. as a symbolic expression of their unconscious conflicts.

This approach gave her a road into the child's unconscious: following closely the transference and the anxieties, as in the analysis of adults, she was able to discover the rich world of the child's unconscious phantasy and object-relations.

Her observations in the playroom gave direct confirmation from child material of Freud's theories of infantile sexuality. However, phenomena could also be observed which were not expected.

The Oedipus complex was thought to start at about three or four years of age, but she observed children of 2½ displaying oedipal phantasies and anxieties which clearly already had a history. Furthermore, pregenital as well as genital trends seemed to be involved in those phantasies and to play an important rôle in oedipal anxieties. In the Oedipus complex of older children, those pregenital trends also seemed to play an important rôle and to contribute significantly to oedipal anxieties. The super-ego appeared much earlier than would have been expected from classical theory, and it seemed to have very savage characteristics—

oral, urethral and anal. Thus for instance, Erna's* maternal super-ego, the "Fisherwoman" and the "Rubber Woman," exhibited the same anal and oral traits as characterized Erna's own sexual phantasies. Rita,* aged $2\frac{3}{4}$, in her pavor nocturnus felt threatened by a mother and father who would bite off her genital and destroy her babies. The fear of these parental imagos paralysed her play and activities. Similarly severe super-egos were exhibited by other patients.

Following the child's symbolization and repetition, in the transference, of earlier object relationships and anxieties, she was led to see that the child's object relationships extend far into the past, right back to a relationship to part-objects, such as the breast and the penis, preceding the relationship to the parents as whole people. She also found that the anxiety stirred by these earliest object relationships may have a lasting influence on the later ones and the form of the Oedipus complex. Those early object relationships were characterized by the importance of phantasy. Not surprisingly, the younger the child the more he was under the sway of omnipotent phantasies, and she was able to follow the complex interplay between the child's unconscious phantasies and his real experience and the gradual way in which the child developed a more realistic relation to his external objects. The conflict between aggression and libido, well known from the analysis of adults, proved to be all the more intense in the early stages of development, and she noticed that the anxiety (in keeping with Freud's later theory of anxiety) is due more to the operation of aggression than that of libido, and that it is primarily against aggression and anxiety that defences were erected. Among those defences denial, splitting, projection and introjection appeared to be active before repression was organized. Melanie Klein saw that little children, under the spur of anxiety, were constantly trying to split their objects and their feelings and trying to retain good feelings and introject good objects, whilst expelling bad objects and projecting bad feelings. Following the fate of the child's object relations and the constant interplay between reality and phantasy,

* Case reported in *The Psycho-Analysis of Children* (1932).

splitting, projection and introjection, she was led to see how the child builds inside himself a complex internal world. The super-ego of course was known as an internal phantasy object; but in seeing how it is gradually built up in the child's internal world, Melanie Klein saw that what was known of the super-ego in the genital stages was but a last stage of a complex development. It could also be seen that not only does the ego have relations of different kinds with its internal objects but that the internal objects themselves are perceived by the child as having relations with one another. Thus, for instance, the child's phantasies about parental sexuality, when the parental couple is introjected, become an important part of the structure of the internal world.

Her work with children and adults, presented in a number of papers as well as in *The Psycho-Analysis of Children*, led her to a formulation of the earliest stages of the Oedipus complex and the super-ego in terms of early object relationships, with an emphasis on anxieties, defences and object relations, part as well as whole.

In the oral-sadistic phase, the child attacks his mother's breast and incorporates it as both destroyed and destructive —"a bad persecuting internal breast." This in Melanie Klein's view is the earliest root of the persecuting and sadistic aspect of the super-ego. Parallel with this introjection, in situations of love and gratification the infant introjects an ideal loved and loving breast which becomes the root of the ego-ideal aspect of the super-ego.

Soon, and partially under the impact of the frustration and anxiety in the breast relationship, the child's desires and phantasies extend to the whole of his mother's body. The mother's body is phantasied as containing all riches including new babies and the father's penis. Since this turning to the mother's body happens at the time when early feelings and phantasies predominate, the infant's first dawning perception of the parental intercourse is of an oral nature and the mother is conceived of as incorporating the father's penis in intercourse. Thus one of the riches of mother's body is this incorporated penis.

The child turns to his mother's body all his libidinal desires but, because of frustration, envy and hatred, also all his destructiveness. These desires also involve objects phantasied inside mother's body, and in relation to them the infant also has greedy libidinal desires and phantasies of scooping them out and devouring them or, because of his hatred and envy, aggressive phantasies of biting, tearing and destroying—as in Erna's phantasy of making "eye salad" of the contents of her mother's body.

Soon, to the oral sadism is added urethral sadism, with phantasies of drowning, cutting and burning, and anal sadism which in the early anal phase is of a predominantly explosive kind and in the later anal phase becomes more secret and poisonous. These attacks on mother's body lead to phantasies of its being a terrifying place full of destroyed and vengeful objects, amongst which father's penis acquires a particular importance.

It is in connection with her understanding of the child's relation to the mother's body that Melanie Klein elucidated the importance of phantasy and unconscious anxiety in the child's relation to the external world and the rôle of symbol-formation in the child's development. When at the height of oral ambivalence, the child penetrates in his phantasy and attacks the mother's body and its contents, her body becomes an object of anxiety, which forces the child to displace his interest from her body to the world around him. Thus through symbolization his interest in his mother's body begins to extend to the whole world around him. A certain amount of anxiety is a necessary spur to this development. If the anxiety is excessive, however, the whole process of symbol-formation comes to a stop. In her paper "The Importance of Symbol-Formation in the Development of the Ego" (1930), Melanie Klein describes a psychotic child, Dick, in whom symbol-formation was severely impeded, as a result of which he failed to endow the world around him with any interest whatsoever. In his case, analysis revealed that his attack on his mother's body led to such severe anxiety that he denied all interest in her and could not therefore symbolize this interest in other objects or relations.

Melanie Klein's description of Dick's phantasy of penetration of his mother's body, accompanied by projection and identification, foreshadows her later formulations of the mechanism of projective identification. She was also the first to notice that in the psychotic process it is the nature of symbol-formation itself which is affected. This aspect of her work had a fundamental influence on later research into the nature of psychotic states.

As the child becomes more aware of the separate identities of his parents and sees them increasingly as a couple engaged in intercourse rather than as a mother incorporating father, the child's desires, and, when in anger and jealousy, his attacks, extend to the parental couple. These attacks are of two kinds: the infant may phantasy himself attacking the parents directly, or he projects his aggression and in his phantasy makes the parents attack one another, giving rise to the experience of the primal scene as a sadistic and terrifying event. Thus the parental couple, like the mother's body, becomes an object of fear.

The child's fear at the height of these phantasies may be twofold: it is both the fear of his external parents and the fear of his internal ones, since first the mother, and then both parents, are introjected, giving rise to terrifying punitive internal imagos. It was in connection with those phantasies that Melanie Klein first drew attention to the importance both of splitting and the interplay of introjection and projection, which she observed as very active mental mechanisms in small children. Faced with the anxiety aroused by the terrifying internal figures, the child tries to split his image of the good parents and his own good and loving feelings from the image of the bad parents and his own destructiveness.

The more sadistic are his phantasies towards the parents, and the more terrifying therefore the imagos of them, the more he feels compelled to keep these feelings away from his good parents and the more he tries to introject again those good external parents. Introjection of bad figures however cannot be avoided. Thus in the early stages of development the infant would introject both the good and the bad breasts, penises, mother's body and parental couple. He tries to deal with the bad introjects which become equated with faeces by anal mechanisms of control and ejection.

In Melanie Klein's view the super-ego not only precedes the Oedipus complex but promotes its development. The anxiety produced by the internalized bad figures makes the child seek all the more desperately libidinal contact with his parents as external objects. There is a desire to possess the mother's body not only for libidinal and aggressive purposes but also out of anxiety to seek reassurance in her real person against the terrifying internal figure. There is also the wish to make restitution and reparation to the real mother in real intercourse for damage done in phantasy. Similarly, with father, the real father and his penis are a reassurance against the terrifying internal introjected penis and father. As a libidinal object, his good penis is sought as a reassurance against the bad internal penis and as a rival the real father is far less terrifying than the internal, distorted representation. Thus the pressure of the anxieties produced by internal objects drives the child towards an oedipal relation to the real parents. At the same time, anxieties of the oral and early anal sadistic stage prompt the child towards abandoning this position for the genital one, which is less sadistic.

Melanie Klein's investigations into the early stages of the Oedipus complex led her to differ in certain important respects from Freud's formulations about female sexuality and the importance of the phallic stage in particular. In her view, the little girl, turning away from the breast to her mother's body, just like the little boy, has phantasies of scooping out and possessing herself of all its contents, particularly of the father's penis inside mother and her babies. Like the little boy, since her phantasies are very ambivalent, the contents of mother's body, including the penis, can be felt as very good or very bad, but under the impact of early frustration and envy she turns more and more to her father's penis, first of all inside her mother's body, then as an external attribute of father's, in an oral incorporative way. Melanie Klein observed that, in the little girl, there is an early awareness of her vagina and the passive oral attitude becomes transferred from the mouth to the vagina, paving the way to a genital oedipal position. In this early attitude to her mother there are elements of both heterosexual and homosexual development. The early mother super-ego may be too terrifying for the little girl to face rivalry with mother, and thus it contributes to homosexuality. Similarly, if her father's penis becomes too bad an object, it may lead to fear of sexual relations with it. Under the impact of guilt and fear, restitutive phantasies in relation to her mother's body may also become a strong determinant of homosexuality. On the other hand, the early desire to take mother's place and possess her riches, the turning to father's penis as an object of desire, restitution, and reparation in relation to the internal mother, and the wish to provide this internal mother with a good penis and babies, all contribute to the heterosexual development.

In relation to the boy's Oedipus complex there was also a certain change of emphasis. The early relation to mother's breast and phantasies about her body in Melanie Klein's view play a significant rôle in the development of the boy's Oedipus complex as well as in the girl's. The early turning away from the breast to the penis happens as in the little girl, laying the foundations for the boy's feminine position; and very early on the little boy, like the little girl, has a struggle between this feminine position in which he turns away from mother to a good paternal penis, and his masculine position in which he wishes to identify with father and desires his mother. The anxieties stirred by his internal objects lead him increasingly to turn his sexual wishes towards his real external mother.

It is not easy to assess what was Melanie Klein's central contribution to psycho-analytical theory and practice at that stage. Her findings about early object relations have certainly thrown a new light on sexuality, both male and female, revealing in both sexes an early awareness of the vagina and the importance of the phantasies in relation to mother's body and its contents. Female sexuality appeared as something in its own right rather than a castrated version of male sexuality, and the boy's feminine position acquired greater importance. She had explored the history of the Oedipus complex and brought out the importance of pregenital stages and part-object relations in the development of both the Oedipus complex and the super-ego. The rôle of aggression underwent a certain revaluation: she described in detail the early conflict between the life and the death instincts, and the anxieties and defences to which it gives rise. The study of the introjected objects threw light, in far greater detail than had been possible before, on the inner structure of the super-ego and the ego.

In her early work she does not conceptually distinguish between anxiety and guilt (except in her paper "The Early Development of Conscience in the Child" (1933)), but sees both as elements promoting the growth of the ego as well as, in pathological cases, its inhibition. The study of the interplay between aggression and libido lead to the observation of the rôle of reparation in psychic life. In her paper "The Importance of Symbol-Formation in the Development of the Ego" (1930) Melanie Klein described the rôle of anxiety and guilt about attacks on the mother's body and the urge to make reparation as an important factor in the creative impulse—a theme which was to be elaborated fully and richly when she came to formulate the characteristics of the depressive position.

Melanie Klein gained access to the understanding of the child's inner structure through following the transference and the symbolism of the child's play. This understanding of the child's play as the symbolization of his phantasies led her to the realization that not only play but all the child's activities—even the most realistically oriented—simultaneously with their reality-function, served to express, contain and canalize the child's unconscious phantasy by means of symbolization. The fundamental rôle played in the child's development by unconscious phantasy and its symbolic expression led her to an extension and a reformulation of the concept of unconscious phantasy.·

BIBLIOGRAPHY

SIGMUND FREUD: *Beyond the Pleasure Principle* (1920), *Standard Edition*, 18 (London: Hogarth).

MELANIE KLEIN: "The role of school in the libidinal development of the child," *Int.J.Psycho-Anal.*, *Vol. 5* (1924).

"Infantile anxiety situations reflected in a work of art," *Int.J. Psycho-Anal.*, *Vol. 10* (1929).

"The importance of symbol formation in the development of the ego," *Int.J.Psycho-Anal.*, *Vol. 11* (1930).

The Psychoanalysis of Children (London: Hogarth, 1932).

CHAPTER TWO

PHANTASY

I HAVE MENTIONED in the last chapter Melanie Klein's observation of the importance of dynamic unconscious phantasy in the child's mental life. The importance she attaches to this led her to broaden and reformulate the concept of unconscious phantasy. I think that clarifying her use of this concept is essential to the understanding of her theories and that it may help to avert many common misunderstandings (for instance, about the nature of "internal objects" or projective identification).

Some psychologists used to object to Freud's description of the mind on the grounds that it was anthropomorphic—a strange objection, it would seem, since psycho-analysis is concerned with describing man. What they meant was that Freud appeared to see mental structure as though it contained objects which were anthropomorphic or man-like, when he described such concepts as the super-ego. Understanding the concept of unconscious phantasy would do much to remove this object. Freud, in his description of the super-ego, is not implying that there is a little man actually contained in our unconscious, but that this is one of the unconscious phantasies which we have about the contents of our body and our psyche. Freud never refers specifically to the super-ego as a phantasy; nevertheless he makes it clear that this part of the personality is due to an introjection—in phantasy—of a parental figure, a parental phantasy figure distorted by the child's own projections.

The same kind of criticism has been levelled by psycho-analysts against the Kleinian description of internal objects.

Equally, these internal objects are not "objects" situated in the body or the psyche: like Freud, Melanie Klein is describing unconscious phantasies which people have about what they contain. In her work, Freud's concept of unconscious phantasy has been very much extended and given more weight. Unconscious phantasies are ubiquitous and always active in every individual. That is to say, their presence is no more indicative of illness or lack of reality-sense than is the presence of the Oedipus complex. What will determine the character of the individual's psychology is the nature of these unconscious phantasies and how they are related to external reality.

Susan Isaacs, in her paper "On the Nature and Function of Phantasy," elaborates Melanie Klein's view on the relation between unconscious phantasy and instincts and mental mechanisms. She states that phantasy may be considered the psychic representative or the mental correlate, the mental expression of instincts. James Strachey, in the editorial notes to Freud's paper "Instincts and their Vicissitudes," draws attention to the fact that Freud wavers between two definitions of instincts. In that paper he describes the instinct as "a concept on the frontier between the mental and the somatic, the psychical representative of the stimuli originating within the organism and reaching the mind," or, in another paper, "the concept on the frontier between the somatic and the mental, the psychical representative of organic forces." Strachey says:

> These accounts seem to make it plain that Freud was drawing no distinction between the instinct and its "psychical representative." He was apparently regarding the instinct itself as the psychical representative of somatic forces. If now, however, we turn to the later papers in the series, we seem to find him drawing a very sharp distinction between the instinct and its psychical representative.

And Strachey goes on to give several references, for instance quoting from the paper on "The Unconscious:"

> An instinct can never become an object of consciousness— only the idea that represents the instinct can. Even in the

unconscious, moreover, an instinct cannot be represented otherwise than by an idea.

It seems to me that Susan Isaacs's way of using the concept of phantasy bridges the gap between the two ways in which Freud viewed instinct. The "ideas" representing the instinct would be the original primitive phantasies. The operation of an instinct in this view is expressed and represented in mental life by the phantasy of the satisfaction of that instinct by an appropriate object. Since instincts operate from birth, some crude phantasy life can be assumed as existing from birth. The first hunger and the instinctual striving to satisfy that hunger are accompanied by the phantasy of an object capable of satisfying that hunger. As phantasies derive directly from instincts on the borderline between the somatic and psychical activity, these original phantasies are experienced as somatic as well as mental phenomena. So long as the pleasure–pain principle is in ascendence, phantasies are omnipotent and no differentiation between phantasy and reality-experience exists. The phantasied objects and the satisfaction derived from them are experienced as physical happenings.

For example, an infant going to sleep, contentedly making sucking noises and movements with his mouth or sucking his own fingers, phantasies that he is actually sucking or incorporating the breast and goes to sleep with a phantasy of having the milk-giving breast actually inside himself. Similarly, a hungry, raging infant, screaming and kicking, phantasies that he is actually attacking the breast, tearing and destroying it, and experiences his own screams which tear him and hurt him as the torn breast attacking him in his own inside. Therefore, not only does he experience a want, but his hunger-pain and his own screams may be felt as a persecutory attack on his inside.

Phantasy-forming is a function of the ego. The view of phantasy as a mental expression of instincts through the medium of the ego assumes a higher degree of ego-organization than is usually postulated by Freud. It assumes that the ego from birth is capable of forming, and indeed is driven by instincts and anxiety to form primitive object-relationships in phantasy and reality. From the moment of birth the infant has to deal with the impact of reality, starting with the experience of birth itself and proceeding to endless experiences of gratification and frustration of his desires. These reality experiences immediately influence and are influenced by unconscious phantasy. Phantasy is not merely an escape from reality, but a constant and unavoidable accompaniment of real experiences, constantly interacting with them.

An example of phantasies influencing the reaction to reality may be seen when a hungry, raging infant, on being offered the breast, instead of accepting it, turns away from it and will not feed. Here the phantasy may be of having attacked and destroyed the breast, which is then felt to have turned bad and to be attacking in its turn. The actual external breast, therefore, when it does return to feed the baby, is not felt as a good feeding breast, but is distorted by these phantasies into a terrifying persecutor. Such phantasies can easily be observed in the play of fairly small children, as well as in the play and speech of slightly older children. They can persist in the unconscious in children and adults, giving rise to feeding difficulties.

Some analysts think that these phantasies arise later and are retrospectively projected into babyhood. This is surely an unnecessary additional hypothesis, especially as there is a marked consistency between what we can observe in infants' behaviour, in phantasies which are actually expressed once the stages of play and speech have been reached, and the analytical material in the consulting room.

In more sophisticated cases it is possible to see how, even though reality may be perceived and observed accurately, unconscious phantasies can determine what kind of causal sequence is attributed to events. The typical example here is the child whose parents actually have a bad and quarrelsome relationship. In analysis, it often transpires that the child feels that this relationship is the result of his own wishes that the parents should quarrel, and that his urinary and faecal attacks have messed up and spoilt the parental relationship.

If unconscious phantasy is constantly influencing and altering the perception or interpretation of reality, the converse also holds true: reality impinges on unconscious phantasy. It is experienced, incorporated and exerts a very strong influence on unconscious phantasy itself. Take, for instance, the infant who is beginning to get hungry and who overcomes hunger by an omnipotent hallucination of having a good feeding breast: his situation will be radically different if he is soon fed from what it will be if he is allowed to remain hungry for a long time. In the first situation the real breast that is offered by the mother will, in the infant's experience, merge with the breast that has been phantasied, and the infant's feeling will be that his own goodness and that of the good object are strong and lasting. In the second case the infant will be overcome by hunger and anger and, in his phantasy, the experience of a bad and persecuting object will become stronger with its implication that his own anger is more powerful than his love and the bad object stronger than the good one.

This aspect of the interrelationship between unconscious phantasy and actual external reality is very relevant when one tries to evaluate the comparative importance of environment on the child's development. Environment has, of course, exceedingly important effects in infancy and childhood, but it does not follow that, without a bad environment, no aggressive and persecutory phantasies and anxieties would exist. The importance of the environmental factor can only be correctly evaluated in relation to what it means in terms of the infant's own instincts and phantasies. As has been stated, it is when the infant has been under the sway of angry phantasies, attacking the breast, that an actual bad experience becomes all the more important, since it confirms, not only his feeling that the external world is bad, but also the sense of his own badness and the omnipotence of his malevolent phantasies. Good experiences, on the other hand, tend to lessen the anger, modify the persecutory experiences and mobilize the baby's love and gratitude and his belief in a good object.

Up to this point emphasis has been laid on the rôle of phantasy as a mental expression of the instincts in contradistinction to the view of phantasy purely as an instrument of defence and a means of escape from external reality. The functions of phantasy, however, are manifold and complicated, and phantasy has a defensive aspect which must be taken into account. Since phantasy aims at fulfilling instinctual drives, irrespective of external reality, gratification derived from phantasy can be regarded as a defence against the external reality of deprivation. It is, however, more than that: it is also a defence against *internal* reality. The individual, producing a phantasy of wish-fulfilment, is not only avoiding frustration and the recognition of an unpleasant external reality, he is also, which is even more important, defending himself against the reality of his own hunger and anger—his internal reality. Phantasies, moreover, may be used as defences against other phantasies. Typical of these are the manic phantasies, whose main purpose is to ward off underlying depressive phantasies. A typical manic phantasy is that of the self containing a devoured ideal object whose "radiance"* falls on the ego; this is a defence against the underlying phantasy of containing an object which is irreparably destroyed and vengeful and whose "shadow"† falls on the ego.

The consideration of the use of unconscious phantasy as a defence raises the problem of establishing what is its exact relation to the mechanisms of defence. Briefly, the distinction lies in the difference between the actual process and its specific, detailed mental representation. For instance, it is possible to say that an individual at a given moment is using the processes of projection and introjection as mechanisms of defence. But the processes themselves will be experienced by him in terms of phantasies which express what he feels himself to be taking in or putting out, the way in which he does this and the results which he feels these actions to have.

* K. Abraham: "A Short Study of the Development of the Libido" (1917).
† S. Freud: "Mourning and Melancholia" (1917), *Standard Edition*, 14, p. 249.

Patients frequently describe their experience of the process of repression, for instance, by speaking of a dam inside them which may burst under the pressure of something like a torrent. What an observer can describe as a mechanism is experienced and described by the person himself as a detailed phantasy.

A more complicated example can be seen in the following material: a patient who had recently begun his analysis was frequently late, often missed sessions, and used regularly to forget large portions of his analysis. Quite useful analytic work could be done for some days and he would then turn up with little conscious memory of the work and no actual effects of it on his personality, as if the whole process and its results had been obliterated. It was quite clear to me and to my patient (and the process could be named), that he was using the mechanisms of splitting and denial as a defence in the analytic situation. One day, he came late, missing exactly half his session, and said that he had lost his way in Loudoun Road, a street near my home, and that this was where he had spent the first half of the session. He associated Loudoun Road with "Loudun Witches;" it seemed as though he had split the analytic situation so that he could preserve a good relationship with me for half the session, while the split-off bad relationship with a "bad" witch analyst was carried on away from me in Loudoun Road. A few days later an opportunity arose of giving this patient an interpretation about his relationship to the breast, and at this point he had a very vivid phantasy. He suddenly saw himself taking a big knife, cutting off my breast and throwing it into the street. The phantasy was so vivid that the patient experienced at that moment quite acute anxiety. It could then be understood that what had been talked about in terms of a process of splitting and denial was in fact experienced by him as an extremely vivid phantasy. The process of splitting was actually felt by him as taking a knife and splitting off—cutting off—one of his analyst's breasts which he threw out into the street, upon which that breast became the "witch" in Loudoun Road. The denial of persecutory feeling in relation to his analysis was experienced as a cutting of the link between the two breasts, the good and the bad one. Following this session, the splitting and denial lessened considerably and he became able to attend his analysis fairly regularly.

This experience, like many others, emphasizes the fact that the interpretation of mechanisms of defence is often ineffective until an opportunity occurs to interpret them so that they are meaningful to the patient in terms of what he actually feels that he does to the analyst in the transference, to his other objects or to parts of his ego, whilst he is using these mechanisms of defence.

Sometimes one can observe this relation between unconscious phantasy and mechanisms of defence very clearly in patients' dreams. Here are two dreams described by a patient during the hour preceding my holiday. In the first dream, the patient was in a dark room which contained two human figures standing close to one another as well as other less well-defined people. The two figures were exactly alike, except that one of them looked drab and dark, while the other was illuminated. The patient was sure that she alone could see the illuminated figure—it was invisible to other people in the dream.

This patient made extensive use of the mechanisms of splitting, denial and idealization. She had the opportunity that same week to see me in a room full of people, a situation unusual for her, and her association with the dream was that the two figures represented myself. One was the person whom everybody could see in the crowded room, but the other one was "her analyst," her special possession. She felt that she was not going to mind the holiday any more than she had minded or had been jealous about seeing me with other people, because she had this special relation to me which was permanently hers alone. In this first dream it is clear that she deals with her jealousy, stirred both by seeing me with other people and the analytic holiday, through splitting and idealization; she has got the illuminated idealized analyst whom no one can take away from her.

In the second dream the patient dreamt that there was a small girl sitting on the floor cutting out paper with a pair of scissors. She was keeping the cut-out piece to herself; the floor was covered with discarded bits of paper which other children were busy collecting. The second dream is another fuller version of the first: it shows how this splitting and idealization were in fact felt by her. The splitting is expressed in the cutting. She is the little girl who has cut out of her analyst the cut-out figure which, like the illuminated figure in the first dream, is her analyst's good part. The people who could only see a drab analyst-figure are represented in the second dream by the children who have nothing but the discarded bits. The splitting seen in the first dream is clearly experienced in the second dream as an attack, an actual cutting of her analyst into an ideal part and a worthless part; and what is represented in the first dream as idealization is experienced in the second dream as stealing and retaining for herself the best cut-out bits of her analyst. The second dream makes it clear that, for this patient, the processes of splitting and idealization were felt as a very aggressive, greedy and guilty activity.

When we consider the relationship between phantasy and the mechanisms of introjection and projection, we can begin to shed some light on the complex relation between unconscious phantasy, mechanisms and mental structure. Susan Isaacs was concerned with discussing the derivation of phantasies from the matrix of the id, and with the relation it bore to mental mechanisms. I shall attempt to establish two further links, the connection between phantasy and personality structure and that between phantasy and higher mental functions like thinking.

Freud described the ego as a "precipitate of abandoned object cathexes."* This precipitate consists of introjected objects. The first of such objects described by Freud himself is the super-ego. The analysis of early projective and introjective object relationships revealed phantasies of objects introjected into the ego from earliest infancy, starting with the introjection of the ideal and the persecutory breasts. To begin with, part objects are introjected, like the breast and, later, the penis; then whole objects like the mother, the father,

---

* S. Freud: *The Ego and the Id* (1923), *Standard Edition*, 19, p. 29.

the parental couple.   The earlier the introjection, the more fantastic are the objects introjected and the more distorted by what has been projected into them.   As development proceeds, and the reality-sense operates more fully, the internal objects approximate more closely to real people in the external world.

With some of these objects, the ego identifies—introjective identification.   They become assimilated into the ego and they contribute to its growth and characteristics.   Others remain as separate internal objects and the ego maintains a relationship with them (the super-ego being such an object). The internal objects are also felt to be in relationship with one another; for instance, the internal persecutors are experienced as attacking the ideal object as well as the ego. Thus, a complex internal world is built up.   The structure of the personality is largely determined by the more permanent of the phantasies which the ego has about itself and the objects that it contains.

The fact that structure is intimately related to unconscious phantasy is extremely important: it is this which makes it possible to influence the structure of the ego and the super-ego through analysis.   It is by analysing the ego's relations with objects, internal and external, and altering the phantasies about these objects, that we can materially affect the ego's more permanent structure.

The following dream, presented by a patient in the first week of his analysis, illustrates the relation between unconscious phantasy, reality, mechanisms of defence and ego structure.   It is certain that this patient had never read any analytical literature and had never heard of these concepts, particularly of the super-ego, otherwise the dream might be viewed with much more scepticism.   The patient, who was a naval officer, dreamt of a pyramid.   At the bottom of this pyramid there was a crowd of rough sailors, bearing a heavy gold book on their heads.   On this book stood a naval officer of the same rank as himself, and on his shoulders an admiral. The admiral, he said, seemed in his own way, to exercise as great a pressure from above and to be as awe-inspiring as the crowd of sailors who formed the base of the pyramid and pressed up from below. Having told this dream, he said: "This is myself, this is my world. The gold book represents a golden mean, a road on which I try to keep. I am squashed between the pressure of my instincts and what I want to do, and the prohibitions coming to me from my conscience." Later associations enabled him to identify the admiral with his father. But this admiral, his father, was very changed from the real father as he remembered him. The fact that this admiral was just as strong and frightening as the sailors, representing the patient's instincts, made it clear that the severity of the super-ego was due here to the projection of his own aggressive instincts into his father. We can see here the interrelation between phantasy and external reality, the reality of the father's personality being altered by projection. His main defence mechanism, repression, is represented in phantasy by the combined pressure of the admiral-super-ego, and the naval officer-ego, trying to keep the instincts under. His personality-structure is also clearly represented by the three layers, the instincts pushing upwards, the super-ego pressing down from above, and his feeling of his ego being squashed and restricted between the two. In this dream we can also clearly see the operation of projection and introjection: he projects his aggression into his father, and the introjection of his father forms his super-ego.

All this—structure and mental mechanisms (projection, introjection and repression)—was presented by the patient himself in his dream. And when he said "This is me—this is my world," he made it clear that he was describing phantasies that he had about himself and his internal world. Phantasy-forming is a primitive function—to understand its importance for the personality one has to see its relevance to higher mental functions such as thinking.

Phantasy belongs originally to functioning, in the terms of the pleasure–pain principle. In "The Two Principles of Mental Functioning" Freud says:

With the introduction of the reality principle, one species of thought-activity was split off; it was kept free from reality-

testing and remained subordinated to the pleasure principle
alone. This activity is *phantasying*.

Thought, on the other hand, was developed in the service of
reality testing, primarily as a means of sustaining tension
and delaying satisfaction. And quoting from the same
paper:

> Thinking was endowed with characteristics which made it
> possible for the mental apparatus to tolerate an increased
> tension of stimulus while the process of discharge was post-
> poned.

(In this view phantasy appears late in the infant's life, after
reality testing has been established.)

Nevertheless, these two mental activities have one important thing in common. They *both* enable the ego to
sustain tension without immediate motor discharge. The
infant capable of sustaining a phantasy is not driven to discharge "as a means of unburdening the mental apparatus of
accretions of stimuli." He can sustain his desire with the help
of phantasy for some time, until satisfaction in reality is avail-
able. If the frustration is severe, or the infant has little
capacity for maintaining his phantasy, the motor discharge
takes place, often accompanied by the disintegration of the
immature ego. So until reality testing and thought processes
are well established, phantasy fulfils in the early mental life
some of the functions later taken over by thinking.

In a footnote to "The Two Principles of Mental Functioning," Freud says:

> It will rightly be objected that an organization which was a
> slave to the pleasure principle and neglected the reality of the
> external world could not maintain itself alive for the shortest
> time, so that it could not have come into existence at all. The
> employment of a fiction like this is, however, justified when
> one considers that the infant—provided one includes with it
> the care it receives from its mother—does almost realize a
> psychical system of this kind.

I emphasize the word "almost" here, because, from very
early on, the healthy infant has some awareness of his needs

and the capacity to communicate them to his mother. From the moment the infant starts interacting with the outer world, he is engaged in testing his phantasies in a reality setting. (This view depends of course on the concept of primitive phantasy preceding the development of thought.) I want to suggest here that the origin of thought lies in this process of testing phantasy against reality; that is, that thought is not only contrasted with phantasy, but is based on it and derived from it.

The reality principle, we know, is but the pleasure principle modified by reality testing. Thinking could be viewed as a modification of unconscious phantasy, a modification similarly brought about by reality testing. The richness, depth and accuracy of a person's thinking will depend on the quality and malleability of his unconscious phantasy life and his capacity to subject it to reality testing.

BIBLIOGRAPHY

W. R. BION: *Learning from Experience* (London: Heinemann, 1964).

SIGMUND FREUD: "Instincts and their Vicissitudes" (1915), *Standard Edition*, 14 (London: Hogarth).

"The Unconscious" (1915), *Standard Edition*, 14 (London: Hogarth).

"Formulations on the Two Principles of Mental Functioning" (1911), *Standard Edition*, 12 (London: Hogarth).

PAULA HEIMANN: "Certain functions of introjection and projection in early infancy," *Developments in Psycho-Analysis* (Chapter 4), Melanie Klein and others (Hogarth, 1952).

SUSAN ISAACS: "The nature and function of phantasy," *Developments in Psycho-Analysis* (Chapter 3), Melanie Klein and others (Hogarth, 1952).

MELANIE KLEIN: "On the development of mental functioning," *Int.J. Psycho-Anal.*, vol. 39 (1958).

JOAN RIVIERE: "On the genesis of psychical conflict in earliest infancy," *Developments in Psycho-Analysis* (Chapter 2), Melanie Klein and others (Hogarth, 1952).

HANNA SEGAL: "Contribution to the Symposium on Phantasy," *Int.J. Psycho-Anal.*, vol. 44 (1963).

CHAPTER THREE

THE PARANOID–SCHIZOID POSITION

IN THE LAST CHAPTER, I suggested that Melanie Klein's use of the concept of unconscious phantasy implies a higher degree of ego organization than that usually assumed by Freud. The controversy among analysts about the state of the ego in the earliest months of infancy is not a matter of mutual misunderstanding or a different use of language. It is an important and real controversy about matters of fact, and naturally any views about what is experienced by the infant must be based on a picture of what his ego is like at any given stage. Any meaningful description of the processes involved must start with a description of the ego.

In Melanie Klein's view, sufficient ego exists at birth to experience anxiety, use defence mechanisms and form primitive object-relations in phantasy and reality. This view is not entirely at variance with Freud's. In some of his concepts he seems to imply the existence of an early ego. He also describes an early defence mechanism, namely the deflection of the death instinct, occurring at the beginning of life, and his concept of hallucinatory wish-fulfilment implies an ego capable of forming a phantasy object relationship.

To assume that the ego has, from the start, the capacity to experience anxiety, use defence mechanisms and form object-relations is not to imply that the ego at birth resembles in any marked degree the ego of a well-integrated infant of six months, let alone that of a child or a fully developed adult.

To begin with, the early ego is largely unorganized,

24

though, in keeping with the whole trend of physiological and psychological growth, it has from the beginning a tendency towards integration. At times, under the impact of the death instinct and intolerable anxiety, this tendency is swept away and defensive disintegration occurs, about which more will be said later. In the earliest stages of development, therefore, the ego is labile, in a state of constant flux, its degree of integration varying from day to day, or even from moment to moment.

The immature ego of the infant is exposed from birth to the anxiety stirred up by the inborn polarity of instincts— the immediate conflict between the life instinct and the death instinct. It is also immediately exposed to the impact of external reality, both anxiety-producing, like the trauma of birth, and life-giving, like the warmth, love and feeding received from its mother. When faced with the anxiety produced by the death instinct, the ego deflects it. This deflection of the death instinct, described by Freud, in Melanie Klein's view consists partly of a projection, partly of the conversion of the death instinct into aggression. The ego splits itself and projects that part of itself which contains the death instinct outwards into the original external object— the breast. Thus, the breast, which is felt to contain a great part of the infant's death instinct, is felt to be bad and threatening to the ego, giving rise to a feeling of persecution. In that way, the original fear of the death instinct is changed into fear of a persecutor. The intrusion of the death instinct into the breast is often felt as splitting it into many bits, so that the ego is confronted with a multitude of persecutors. Part of the death instinct remaining in the self is converted into aggression and directed against the persecutors.

At the same time, a relation is established with the ideal object. As the death instinct is projected outwards, to ward off the anxiety aroused by containing it, so the libido is also projected, in order to create an object which will satisfy the ego's instinctive striving for the preservation of life. As with the death instinct, so with the libido. The ego projects part of it outwards, and the remainder is used to establish a libidinal relationship to this ideal object. Thus, quite early, the ego has a relationship to two objects; the primary object, the breast, being at this stage split into two parts, the ideal breast and the persecutory one. The phantasy of the ideal object merges with, and is confirmed by, gratifying experiences of love and feeding by the real external mother, while the phantasy of persecution similarly merges with real experiences of deprivation and pain, which are attributed by the infant to the persecutory objects. Gratification, therefore, not only fulfils the need for comfort, love and nourishment, but is also needed to keep terrifying persecution at bay; and deprivation becomes not merely a lack of gratification, but a threat of annihilation by persecutors. The infant's aim is to try to acquire, to keep inside and to identify with the ideal object, seen as life-giving and protective, and to keep out the bad object and those parts of the self which contain the death instinct. The leading anxiety in the paranoid–schizoid position is that the persecutory object or objects will get inside the ego and overwhelm and annihiliate both the ideal object and the self. These features of the anxiety and object-relationships experienced during this phase of development led Melanie Klein to call it the paranoid–schizoid position, since the leading anxiety is paranoid, and the state of the ego and its objects is characterized by the splitting, which is schizoid.

Against the overwhelming anxiety of annihilation, the ego evolves a series of mechanisms of defence, a defensive use of introjection and projection probably being the first. We have seen that, as an expression of instincts as well as a defence measure, the ego strives to introject the good and to project the bad. This, however, is not the only use of introjection and projection. There are situations in which the good is projected, in order to keep it safe from what is felt to be overwhelming badness inside, and situations in which persecutors are introjected and even identified with in an attempt to gain control of them. The permanent feature is that in situations of anxiety the split is widened and projection and introjection are used in order to keep persecutory and ideal objects as far as possible from one another, while keeping both of them under control. The situation may fluctuate rapidly, and persecutors may be felt now outside, giving a feeling of external threat, now inside, producing fears of a hypochondriacal nature.

Splitting is linked with increasing idealization of the ideal object, in order to keep it far apart from the persecutory object and make it impervious to harm. Such extreme idealization is also connected with magic omnipotent denial. When persecution is too intense to be borne, it may be completely denied. Such magic denial is based on a phantasy of the total annihilation of the persecutors. Another way in which omnipotent denial may be used against excessive persecution is by idealizing the persecuting object itself, and treating it as ideal. Sometimes the ego identifies with this pseudo-ideal object.

This kind of idealization and omnipotent denial of persecution is often seen in the analysis of schizoid patients, who present a history of having been "perfect babies," never protesting and never crying, as though all experiences were experienced by them as good ones. In adult life, these mechanisms lead to lack of discrimination between good and bad and to fixations upon bad objects that have to be idealized.

From the original projection of the death instinct there evolves another mechanism of defence, extremely important in this phase of development, namely, projective identification. In projective identification parts of the self and internal objects are split off and projected into the external object, which then becomes possessed by, controlled and identified with the projected parts.

Projective identification has manifold aims: it may be directed towards the ideal object to avoid separation, or it may be directed towards the bad object to gain control of the source of danger. Various parts of the self may be projected, with various aims: bad parts of the self may be projected in order to get rid of them as well as to attack and destroy the object, good parts may be projected to avoid separation or to keep them safe from bad things inside or to improve the external object through a kind of primitive projective re-

paration. Projective identification starts when the paranoid–
schizoid position is first established in relation to the breast,
but it persists and very often becomes intensified when the
mother is perceived as a whole object and the whole of her
body is entered by projective identification.

An example taken from the analysis of a little girl of five
illustrates some aspects of projective identification. Towards
the end of a session which took place a few weeks before a long
break, she started spreading glue on the floor of the playroom
and on her shoes. She was at that time particularly preoccupied with pregnancies. I interpreted that she wanted
to glue herself to the floor so as not to be sent away at the
end of the session which represented the interruption of her
treatment. She confirmed this interpretation verbally and
then proceeded to smear the glue in a more messy and dirty
fashion, saying with great satisfaction "But it's also a 'sick'
right on your floor." I interpreted that she wanted to glue
herself not only to the inside of the room, but also to the inside
of my body where new babies grew, and to mess it and dirty
it with the "sick." The next day she brought me a big
red geranium. She pointed to the stem and the plentiful
buds round it and said "Do you see? All those babies come
out of the stem. This is a present for you." I interpreted
that now she wanted to give me the penis and all the little
babies that come out of it to make up for what she felt was
the mess that she had made of my babies and the inside of
my body the previous day.

Some time later in the session the patient took up the
glue again and said she was going to draw an animal on
the floor—a "foxglove." Then she hesitated and said
"No, the foxglove is a flower." What she really meant
was a fox. She didn't know what the flower she had given
me was called. "It may be a foxglove, too." As she painted
the fox on the floor, using glue as her paint, she went on
chatting about foxes. "They creep in without anybody
noticing. They have big mouths and teeth and eat up little
chicks and eggs." She also said, with great satisfaction,
"This one was a very slippery fox since nobody would see
it on the floor and people would slip and break their legs."

So the "foxglove" flower which she had offered me was an expression of the "slippery fox" part of her personality. It was the bad, damaging "slippery fox" part of herself (which was also identified with her father's penis) which she wanted to slip into me so that it should continue to live inside me and destroy my eggs and my babies. In doing so she succeeded in getting rid of a part of herself which she did not like and about which she felt guilty, and at the same time, in phantasy, she got possession of her analyst-mother's body, and destroyed the other babies just as she had been doing with her "sick" in the previous session. Since she had got rid of the bad part of herself, she could feel that she was good, the good little girl offering her analyst a flower, while actually she was covertly harming her. The "slippery fox," which no one could see, thus also became a symbol of her hypocrisy.

In the next session she was rather frightened of entering the room; she came in cautiously, tested the floor and was very reluctant to open her drawer. This was unusual behaviour at that stage of her analysis and reminiscent of an earlier period when she was frightened of the toy lion in her drawer. The phantasy involved in projective identi-fication was very real to her. The day after she had painted the slippery fox, the playroom and the drawer—standing for my body—had become a place containing a dangerous animal. When this was interpreted to her, she admitted that she had had a nightmare in which a big animal appeared. Her anxiety lessened, and she opened her drawer.

Up to that point I was felt to contain a dangerous part of herself from which she now felt completely dissociated; her associations with her dream also showed that very soon afterwards I had actually become the dangerous fox myself. This was shown later in the session when she said that the dangerous animal in her dream had "spectacles, like you do, and the same big mouth."

In the above example, projective identification is used as a defence against an impending separation and as a means of controlling the object and of attacking rivals—the unborn babies. The projected part, the "sick" and the "slippery fox" is predominantly the bad, greedy and destructive part, the "slippery fox" being also identified with the bad introjected penis forming the basis of a bad homosexual relationship. As a result of this projection, the analyst, to begin with, was felt as containing and being controlled by this bad part and gradually became totally identified with it.

When the mechanisms of projection, introjection, splitting, idealization, denial and projective and introjective identification fail to master anxiety, and the ego is invaded by it, then disintegration of the ego may occur as a defensive measure. The ego fragments and splits itself into little bits in order to avoid the experience of anxiety. This mechanism, grossly damaging to the ego, usually appears combined with projective identification, the fragmented parts of the ego being immediately projected. This type of projective identification, if used at all extensively, is pathological and will be dealt with more fully in the next chapter.

Various mechanisms of defence are used to protect the infant from experiencing the fear of death from within, to begin with, and from persecutors, external or internal, when the death instinct is deflected. They all, however, produce in turn anxieties of their own. For instance, the projection of bad feelings and bad parts of the self outwards produces external persecution. The reintrojection of persecutors gives rise to hypochondriacal anxiety. The projection of good parts outwards produces the anxiety of being depleted of goodness and of being invaded by persecutors. Projective identification produces a variety of anxieties. The two most important are these: the fear that an attacked object will retaliate equally by projection; and the anxiety of having parts of oneself imprisoned and controlled by the object into which they have been projected. This last anxiety is particularly strong when good parts of the self have been projected, producing a feeling of having been robbed of these good parts and of being controlled by other objects.

Disintegration is the most desperate of all the ego's attempts to ward off anxiety: in order to avoid suffering anxiety the ego does its best not to exist, an attempt which gives rise to a specific acute anxiety—that of falling to bits and becoming atomized.

The following material, presented by a non-psychotic patient, shows certain of these schizoid mechanisms. The patient, a middle-aged lawyer, started the session by re-marking that I was a few minutes late. He added that on the few occasions when this had happened before, he had noticed that I was either late for the first session in the morning or for the session following the lunch break. He said that if I were late, therefore, it was because my own leisure en-croached on the analytical session. He himself was never late for a client because of some private occupation of his own, but he was very frequently late because he allowed one client's time to over-run the next client's time. In this context he made it quite clear that he felt that my behaviour in this respect was more commendable than his; and he made several remarks about his inability to face his clients' aggression and therefore his inability to end their interviews on time. We were both fairly familiar with his inability to manage his affairs, as well as with his feeling of injured innocence that he never did anything for his own sake—it was invariably some of his clients interfering with others. Soon after these comments, he said that he had had a dream which actually had to do with being late. He said that he dreamt about "smokers." (In the fairly recent past, this patient had some professional dealings with delinquents, in which he behaved in a very omnipotent way. These dealings brought him a fair amount of success and money, but subsequently he felt that his success was shabby, and he felt both guilty and ashamed. Some of these delinquent clients were heavy smokers and he occasionally referred to them as "the smokers.")

The dream was that his flat and the adjoining office were invaded by crowds of smokers. They smoked and drank all over the place and made it extremely untidy: they wanted his company and made constant demands on him. Suddenly in the dream he became aware that there was a client in his waiting room to whom he had given an appointment at a certain time, and he realized that he would not be able to

see this client because of the smokers who had invaded his
flat. In angry desperation, he began to shoo the smokers
away and throw them out so that he could see his client
on time. He added that his feeling, now that he was relating
the dream, was that he probably managed to get the smokers
out of the flat and he thinks he managed to see his client
on time. At some point in the dream his wife came in and
told him that she had kept his appointment with his analyst
instead of him, since it was quite clear that he could not
cope with the smokers and with his client who was in the
waiting room and also come to his session on time. This,
in the dream, depressed him considerably. His associations
to the dream were particularly about the smokers. He commented on the greedy, unrestrained way in which the smokers
smoked and drank, on their untidiness, dirt, ruthlessness,
and on the mess they made of his flat. He was sure that
these smokers represented that part of himself which, with
its greed for success, money and cheap satisfaction, messed
up his life and his analysis.

In his associations, however, genuine though they were,
there was one glaring omission: he did not refer to the fact
that I was a fairly heavy smoker, though this had frequently
entered his analysis, the "smokers" in the past often
representing me as a dangerous phallic woman.

The details of the session that followed are not stated
here because the dream in itself is very clear and it is the
theoretical aspect of the dream—the illustration of certain
mechanisms—with which we are concerned. The smokers
stood primarily for a part of myself. In the dream the
patient's object, myself standing for the parental figure,
was split. On the one hand there was the analyst to whom
he wanted to go for his session; on the other hand there was
the crowd of smokers which invaded his flat and prevented
his coming. In so far as I was a good object, I was represented
as one figure, his analyst, and possibly also as the one client
who waited in his waiting room and with whom he felt he
could deal. The bad part of me, however, was not represented
by one smoker, but by a whole crowd of smokers. That is,
the bad object was perceived as being split into a multitude

of persecuting fragments. The split between my good aspect and the smoker's aspect was maintained so rigidly that, in his own associations, the patient did not connect the smokers with me.

This split in the patient's object was accompanied by, and in fact produced by, a split in his own ego. The good part was represented by the patient who, in the dream, wanted to come to his session—also the patient who, as a good lawyer, wanted to see his own client on time. The bad part of himself, which was uncontrolled, greedy, demanding, ambitious and messing-up, he could not tolerate. He split it into a multiplicity of bits and projected it into me, thereby splitting me also into a multitude of little bits; and since he could not stand the resulting persecution and the loss of his good analyst, he further split off the bad fragmented part of me and displaced this on to "the smokers"—thereby partly preserving me as a good object.

This material makes it quite clear why he could never manage his practice and clients. His clients were not in fact felt by him to be people. Each client represented to him split-off bits of a bad parental figure for which I stood in the transference. This figure contained split-off and projected bits of himself. In fact, he could no more deal with his clients than he had been able to deal with these bad parts of himself.

In the light of his dream, it also becomes clear why my being late after my own leisure time was felt by the patient as commendable behaviour as compared with his only being late when it was someone else's fault, though it is also in keeping with his denial of my real dereliction in being late. What he was trying to convey was that he felt I was able to take the responsibility for my own bad behaviour without projecting it. I could express my greed, my uncontrollability or my aggression, so he felt, and could also take full responsibility for it; whereas he felt that he was so greedy, so destructive and so messing-up that he could not take responsibility for controlling this part of himself and had to project it on to other people, for the most part on to his clients.

This dream shows a number of schizoid mechanisms;

the splitting of the object and of the self into a good and a bad part; the idealization of the good object and the splitting into little fragments of the bad part of the self; the projection of bad parts into the object with the resulting feeling of being persecuted by a multitude of bad objects. The method of projecting bad parts of the self split into many fragments, typical of schizoid defences, was characteristic of the patient. He once dreamt that he was facing scores of little Japanese men—his enemies. His associations showed that the Japanese represented his urine and faeces into which he put parts of himself which he wanted to be rid of—urine and faeces were then projected into his objects. On another occasion he wrote an article for a foreign paper which, as he came to realize in his analysis, he felt would have a very bad moral effect on his readers. He consoled himself with the fact that it was "far away" and the consequences could not, therefore, reach him. In a later dream, the article was represented as "a little bit of shit in China."

This patient used schizoid mechanisms mainly as a defence against anxieties of the depressive position, particularly guilt, but the defence in the dream about the smokers was only partially successful because the projection of his bad impulses into the smokers was not complete. Even in the dream itself, the patient felt himself responsible for the smokers, guilty about his relation to his client in the waiting-room and to myself and acutely aware of the feeling of loss of his good object.

Such guilt, however, as he felt in the dream was not felt directly in relation to his greed, ambition, etc. It was felt as guilt about his weakness; this he stated at the beginning of the session, saying that he was always late because of his weakness in dealing with his clients. This weakness, which was consciously and strongly felt, was related to the projection of the aggressive part of himself outside, which made him feel helpless in the face of persecution by the projected bits of himself, which he could not disown, and at the same time made him feel weak and helpless because he felt that his ego had been depleted by the projection even of what he felt to be bad parts of himself.

In describing the paranoid–schizoid position, I have emphasized the anxieties and the defences associated with them. This could give a misleading picture of the infant's early months. It has to be remembered that a normal infant does not spend most of his time in a state of anxiety. On the contrary, in favourable circumstances, he spends most of his time sleeping, feeding, experiencing real or hallucinatory pleasures and thus gradually assimilating his ideal object and integrating his ego. But all infants have periods of anxiety, and the anxieties and defences which are the nucleus of the paranoid–schizoid position are a normal part of human development.

No experience in human development is ever cast aside or obliterated; we must remember that in the most normal individual there will be some situations which will stir up the earliest anxieties and bring into operation the earliest mechanisms of defence. Furthermore, in a well-integrated personality, all stages of development are included, none are split off and rejected; and certain achievements of the ego in the paranoid–schizoid position are indeed very important for later development, for which they lay the foundations. They have a rôle to play in the most mature and integrated personality.

One of the achievements of the paranoid–schizoid position is splitting. It is splitting which allows the ego to emerge out of chaos and to order its experiences. This ordering of experience which occurs with the process of splitting into a good and bad object, however excessive and extreme it may be to begin with, nevertheless orders the universe of the child's emotional and sensory impressions and is a pre-condition of later integration. It is the basis of what is later to become the faculty of discrimination, the origin of which is the early differentiation between good and bad. There are other aspects of splitting which remain and are important in mature life. For instance, the ability to pay attention, or to suspend one's emotion in order to form an intellectual judgment, would not be achieved without the capacity for temporary reversible splitting.

Splitting is also the basis for what later becomes repression.

If early splitting has been excessive and rigid, later repression is likely to be of an excessive neurotic rigidity. When early splitting has been less severe, repression will be less crippling, and the unconscious will remain in better communication with the conscious mind.

So splitting, provided it is not excessive and does not lead to rigidity, is an extremely important mechanism of defence which not only lays the foundations for later and less primitive mechanisms, like repression, but continues to function in a modified form throughout life.

With splitting are connected persecutory anxiety and idealization. Of course both, if retained in their original form in adulthood, distort judgment, but some elements of persecutory anxiety and idealization are always present and play a rôle in adult emotions. Some degree of persecutory anxiety is a precondition for being able to recognize, appreciate and react to actual situations of danger in external conditions. Idealization is the basis of the belief in the goodness of objects and of oneself, and is a precursor of good object-relationships. The relationship to a good object usually contains some degree of idealization, and this idealization persists in many situations such as falling in love, appreciating beauty, forming social or political ideals— emotions which, though they may not be strictly rational, add to the richness and variety of our lives.

Projective identification, too has its valuable aspects. To begin with, it is the earliest form of empathy and it is on projective as well as introjective identification that is based the capacity to "put oneself into another person's shoes." Projective identification also provides the basis of the earliest form of symbol-formation. By projecting parts of itself into the object and identifying parts of the object with parts of the self, the ego forms its first most primitive symbols.

We must, therefore, look at the mechanisms of defence used in the paranoid–schizoid position not only as mechanisms of defence which protect the ego from immediate and overwhelming anxieties, but also as gradual steps in development.

This brings us to the question of how the normal individual grows out of the paranoid–schizoid position. For the paranoid–schizoid position to yield gradually, and in a smooth and relatively undisturbed way, to the next step in development, the depressive position, the necessary precondition is that there should be a predominance of good over bad experiences. To this predominance both internal and external factors contribute.

When there is a predominance of good experience over bad experience, the ego acquires a belief in the prevalence of the ideal object over the persecutory objects, and also of the predominance of its own life instinct over its own death instinct. These two beliefs, in the goodness of the object and in the goodness of the self, go hand in hand, since the ego continually projects its own instincts outwards, thereby distorting the objects, and also introjects its objects, identifying with them. The ego repeatedly identifies with the ideal object, thereby acquiring greater strength and greater capacity to cope with anxieties without recourse to violent mechanisms of defence. The fear of the persecutors lessens and the split between persecutory and ideal objects lessens as well. The persecutors and the ideal objects are allowed to come closer together, and thus to be more ready for integration. Simultaneously the splitting in the ego lessens when the ego feels stronger, with a greater flow of libido. It is more closely related to an ideal object, and less afraid of its own aggression and the anxiety that it stirs up, and the good and bad parts of the ego are allowed to come closer together. At the same time as splitting lessens and the ego has a greater tolerance in relation to its own aggression, the necessity for projection lessens and the ego is more and more able to tolerate its own aggression, to feel it as a part of itself, and is not driven constantly to project it into its objects. In this way, the ego is preparing for integrating its objects, integrating itself, and, through lessening of projective mechanisms, there is a growing differentiation between what is self and what is object. Thus the way to the depressive position is paved. It is, however, very different if there is a predominance of bad experiences over good ones, a situation I shall describe in dealing with the psycho-pathology of the paranoid–schizoid position.

BIBLIOGRAPHY

MELANIE KLEIN: "Notes on some Schizoid Mechanisms," *Developments in Psycho-analysis* (Chapter 9). *Int.J.Psycho-Anal.*, vol. 27 (1946), Melanie Klein and others.
    "On Identification," *New Directions in Psycho-analysis* (Chapter 13), Melanie Klein and others; *Our Adult World and Other Essays* (Chapter 3), Melanie Klein.
HANNA SEGAL: "Some Schizoid Mechanisms Underlying Phobia Formation." *Int.J.Psycho-Anal.*, vol. 35 (1954).

CHAPTER FOUR

ENVY

IN THE PRECEDING CHAPTER, I said that it is essential for the infant's favourable development in the paranoid–schizoid position that good experiences should predominate over bad ones. What the infant's actual experience is depends on both external and internal factors. External deprivation, physical or mental, prevents gratification; but even when the environment is conducive to gratifying experiences, they may still be modified or even prevented by internal factors.

Melanie Klein describes early envy as one such factor, operating from birth and materially affecting the infant's earliest experiences. Envy, of course, has long been recognized in psycho-analytical theory and practice as a most important emotion. Freud, particularly, paid a great deal of attention to penis-envy in women. The significance of other kinds of envy, however—man's envy of another's potency or man's envy of the female possessions or position, women's envy of one another—has not been so specifically recognized. In analytical literature, and in the description of cases, envy plays an important part, but, with the exception of the special case of penis-envy, there is a tendency to confuse envy with jealousy. Interestingly enough, in analytical writing one finds the same confusion as in everyday speech, where envy is commonly called jealousy. On the other hand, it is very rare indeed for jealousy to be described as envy; everyday speech—and this is reflected too in analytical speech—seems to avoid the concept of envy and tends to replace it by that of jealousy.

Melanie Klein, in *Envy and Gratitude* makes a proper distinction between the emotions of envy and jealousy. She considers envy to be the earlier of the two, and shows that envy is one of the most primitive and fundamental emotions. Early envy has to be differentiated from jealousy and from greed.

Jealousy is based on love and aims at the possession of the loved object and the removal of the rival. It pertains to a triangular relationship and therefore to a time of life when objects are clearly recognized and differentiated from one another. Envy, on the other hand, is a two-part relation in which the subject envies the object for some possession or quality; no other live object need enter into it. Jealousy is necessarily a whole-object relationship, whilst envy is essentially experienced in terms of part-objects, though it persists into whole-object relationships.

Greed aims at the possession of all the goodness that can be extracted from the object, regardless of consequences; this may result in the destruction of the object and the spoiling of its goodness, but the destruction is incidental to the ruthless acquirement. Envy aims at being as good as the object, but, when this is felt as impossible, it aims at spoiling the goodness of the object, to remove the source of envious feelings. It is this spoiling aspect of envy that is so destructive to development, since the very source of goodness that the infant depends on is turned bad, and good introjections, therefore, cannot be achieved. Envy, though arising from primitive love and admiration, has a less strong libidinal component than greed and is suffused with the death instinct. As it attacks the source of life, it may be considered to be the earliest direct externalization of the death instinct. Envy stirs as soon as the infant becomes aware of the breast as a source of life and good experience; the real gratification which he experiences at the breast, reinforced by idealization, so powerful in early infancy, makes him feel that the breast is the source of all comforts, physical and mental, an inexhaustible reservoir of food and warmth, love, understanding and wisdom. The blissful experience of satisfaction which this wonderful object can give will increase his love and his desire to possess, preserve and protect it, but the same experience stirs in him also the wish to be himself the source of such perfection; he experiences painful feelings of envy which carry with them the desire to spoil the qualities of the object which can give him such painful feelings.

Envy can fuse with greed, making for a wish to exhaust the object entirely, not only in order to possess all its goodness but also to deplete the object purposefully so that it no longer contains anything enviable. It is the admixture of envy which often makes greed so spoiling and so apparently intractable in analytic treatment. But envy does not stop at exhausting the external object. The very nourishment that has been taken in, so long as it is perceived as having been part of the breast, is in itself an object of envious attacks, which are turned upon the internal object as well. Envy operates also by projection and often mainly so. When the infant feels himself to be full of anxiety and badness and the breast to be the source of all goodness, in his envy he wishes to spoil the breast by projecting into it bad and spoiling parts of himself; thus, in phantasy, the breast is attacked by spitting, urinating, defaecating, passing of wind, and by projective, penetrating looking (the evil eye). As development proceeds, these attacks are continued in relation to the mother's body and her babies, and the parental relationship. In cases of pathological development in the Oedipus complex, envy of the parental relationship plays a more important rôle than true feelings of jealousy.

If early envy is very intense, it interferes with the normal operation of schizoid mechanisms. The process of splitting into an ideal and a persecutory object, so important in the paranoid–schizoid position, cannot be maintained, since it is the ideal object which gives rise to envy and is attacked and spoiled. This leads to confusion between the good and the bad interfering with splitting. As splitting cannot be maintained and an ideal object cannot be preserved, introjection of an ideal object and identification with it is severely interfered with. And with it the development of the ego must necessarily suffer. Strong feelings of envy lead to despair. An ideal object cannot be found, therefore there is no hope of love or help from anywhere. The destroyed objects are the source of endless persecution and later guilt. At the same time, the lack of good introjection deprives the ego of its capacity for growth and assimilation, which would lessen the feeling of the tremendous gap between itself and the object, and a vicious circle arises, in which envy prevents good introjection and this in turn increases envy.

Powerful unconscious envy often lies at the root of negative therapeutic reactions and interminable treatments; one can observe this in patients who have a long history of failed previous treatments. It appeared clearly in a patient who came to analysis after many years of varied psychiatric and psycho-therapeutic treatments. Each course of treatment would bring about an improvement, but deterioration would set in after its termination. When he began his analysis, it soon appeared that the main problem was the strength of his negative therapeutic reaction. I represented mainly a successful and potent father, and his hatred of and rivalry with this figure was so intense that the analysis, representing my potency as an analyst, was unconsciously attacked and destroyed over and over again. On the face of it, it looked like a straightforward oedipal rivalry with the father; but an important element was missing in this oedipal situation, namely, any strong love for, or attraction to women. Women were desirable as possessions of the father and seemed not to be valued for themselves. If he could own them, he would in his mind spoil and destroy them in the same way as he tried to spoil and destroy his father's other possessions, such as his penis or his achievements. In those circumstances, he could not introject his father's potency and identify with it, and he could not introject, preserve or make use of my interpretations.

In the first year of his analysis, he dreamt that he put into the boot of his little car tools belonging to my car (bigger than his), but when he arrived at his destination and opened the boot, all the tools were shattered. This dream symbolized his type of homosexuality; he wanted to take the paternal penis into his anus and steal it, but in the process of doing so, his hatred of the penis, even when introjected, was such that he would shatter it and be unable to make use of it. In the same way, interpretations which he felt as complete and helpful were immediately torn to pieces and disintegrated, so that it was particularly following good sessions which brought relief that he would start to feel confused and persecuted as the fragmented, distorted, half-remembered interpretations confused and attacked him internally. Soon envious attacks were encountered in relation to the parental couple—any union between two people, whatever its character and whatever the sex of the couple, represented to him the envied parental intercourse which had to be attacked and destroyed. This led to a difficulty in retaining a meaningful link with me or, internally, a link between thoughts, ideas and feelings. As his analysis proceeded, the maternal transference came more to the fore with desperate envy in relation to the maternal figure, the female genitalia and orgasm, pregnancy and, particularly, breasts.

One of his long standing symptoms was his inability to eat in company and, particularly, to eat food prepared by his wife. He frequently suffered from delusions that his food was contaminated and poisoned or spoiled by being left too long out of the 'fridge. If his wife or housekeeper spoke whilst he was eating, he felt it as a biting attack on himself and would immediately develop acute gastric pain. In the transference he always felt that I was siding with his wife, ignoring her aggressiveness, and that by interpreting to him I repeated his wife's attacks on him. It soon became clear that the woman who fed him, even when she was gratifying him, was an object of such envy that her food was immediately attacked with urine and faeces and therefore was contaminated as soon as it came into touch with him.

These envious attacks on his good objects, father, parental couple, the feeding mother, interfered with all his introjective processes. As a result, he suffered from difficulties in learning, thinking, working and feeding. His intellectual difficulties were particularly painful to him, since, in keeping with his envious character, he suffered from quite immoderate ambition, which he could never fulfil.

All these problems came to a head when, following several years of analysis and considerable improvement, he had for the first time to present some results of his laboratory research to his colleagues. In his mind this was a world-shaking event. He hoped that his research would shatter and fill with envy the head of his department, whom he admired and envied enormously. At the same time he was terrified of becoming an object of ridicule and contempt. In the transference, at times, the coming event was seen as a great success, devised to show me that he was far more creative than I was and to fill me with envy; at times it was to be a complete disaster which would demonstrate to the world what damage I had done to him and would discredit me for ever. At the same time he was aware that he could not complete and present his work without analytical help and he would try to put me again, as he said, "on your pedestal," and identify with me. At those times the work was felt as being done by me inside him.

A few days before the date on which he was to present his work, I had been able to point out to him that in fact he seemed unable to visualize the meeting or to foresee realistically what reception his work would have. He then realized that he could not do this because he felt that either way it would end in madness. He knew that the idea of a moderate success did not exist for him. If his research was successful—and one word of praise from anyone would be sufficient for him to feel that his research was the most important work ever done on the subject—he was afraid that there would be no holding back his grandiosity and that he would go mad with grandiose delusions. On the other hand, lack of success—and again, a single critical comment would, he knew, be taken by him as complete disaster—would lead to such depression and persecution that he would commit suicide.

The next day he reported the following dream: He was walking in London hand in hand with a dinosaurus; London was quite empty, there wasn't a soul abroad. The dinosaurus was hungry and greedy and the patient kept feeding him with bits from his pocket, in great anxiety lest, when the food was finished, the dinosaurus would eat him up. He thought that maybe London was empty because the dinosaurus had already eaten up all the other inhabitants. The first association was that the dinosaurus must stand for his unlimited vanity. He connected the dream with the end of the previous session and thought that it represented his dilemma in relation to his work. He had to feed his vanity or it would kill him, but, if he fed it, it would only grow bigger and become all the more dangerous. His vanity was the obverse side of his envy, an expression of it as well as a defence against it. It had produced a vacuum around him since all his objects were devoured by it and it was a constant threat to his own life. Further associations with the dream made it clear that he felt that if he tried to satisfy his envy he was tortured by loneliness, remorse, guilt and persecution, and his envy grew because he was unhappy. If he did not satisfy it, he was filled with a destructive devouring envy that destroyed and poisoned him.

Since strong envy in relationship to the primary object gives rise to such acute pain and hopelessness, powerful defences are mobilized against it. Spoiling, which I described as an aim of envy, is partly a defence against it, since a spoiled object arouses no envy. It may be muted to devaluation, in order to protect the object from total spoiling by merely lessening its value. This spoiling or devaluation is usually connected with the powerful projection of envious feelings into the object.

In contrast to devaluation and the projection of envy, rigid idealization may be resorted to, in an attempt to preserve some ideal object. Such idealization, however, is most precarious, since the more ideal the object, the more intense the envy. All these defences contribute to the crippling of the ego.

These defences were very clear in the patient described above. For instance, further analysis of the dinosaurus dream showed that the dinosaurus also represented myself, standing for the internalized father. When the patient felt at all successful, he felt that he was filling his objects with his own monstrous envy. Thus, his superego was felt to be envious and spoiling, attacking all his work, achievements and such goodness as he possessed.

At the same time, the patient tried to protect himself in this desperate situation by some attempt at splitting and idealization. Somewhere in his material there always appeared an idealized object that he could introject and partly identify with. This object altered and changed rapidly. The idealization, however, was subject to one essential condition: this was that the ideal object had to be felt as being not only owned but created by himself. Basically, the only ideal object was an internal breast which he felt had originally been created by him. This phantasy, particularly, accounted for the inordinate length of all his psychiatric treatments. He needed an external object that would keep him wholly and uninterruptedly gratified; under these conditions he could phantasy that he himself was the source of food, and the external object could be completely denied or disparaged. Any frustration would make him aware that it was the mother's breast and not himself that was the source of life and food, and this would immediately lead to devastating attacks. For instance, during one session he proved to himself that I had completely deteriorated (the deterioration of his objects was an ever-recurring phantasy), that I was no good as a psycho-analyst and that probably my career was at an end. I was, according to him, "in the gutter." That same day he came across a reference to my work in a popular magazine. This seemed to upset him, but only for a very short time. Two sessions later he was praising the analysis and my work in a way he had never done before. He was himself surprised at this change and kept wondering why he idealized me so much and why he had put me on "such a pedestal." Then it became clear that, in his phantasy, the fact that I had been mentioned in the article was all right because he felt that it was he who, by idealizing me, had done it; he had put me "on this pedestal." I was allowed to be ideal since he needed me as an ideal object to counteract his internal destructiveness; but only on condition that he could omnipotently either drag me into "the gutter" or elevate me on to "a pedestal." In identification with this ideal object created by himself he felt omnipotent and grandiose. His moods varied between depths of depression, when he felt that everything inside him was destroyed by his envious attacks, and elated moods of grandiosity.

In that very disturbed patient we can see both how the defences against envy contribute to psychopathological development, and how unsuccessful they are in preventing the destructive operation of envy. This is not so in the case of people who are less ill. The defences against envy may be far more successful. For instance, envious feelings and phantasies may be split off early in development, and the ego may be strong enough to prevent their re-emergence. I should like, therefore, to contrast the material I have just presented with that of a far less disturbed patient, to illustrate the working of envy and the defences against it in a better adjusted personality.

This patient was a middle-aged woman, happily married, working in a profession in which she had an absorbing interest and in which she was successful. She came to analysis because of a tendency to depression and an inhibition in work. She worked in an academic profession and, though successful in her career, she found recurring blocks in relation to the more creative and rewarding research aspects of her work.

She presented none of the obvious manifestations of envy, she had no inhibitions in taking in and learning, and was capable of fruitful co-operation with her colleagues. In the transference, there were no overt manifestations of negative therapeutic reaction, and her analytical progress seemed smooth. Envy of the mother did not appear very much; and though feelings of rivalry were intense and led to marked reactions of guilt, they were invariably linked with triangular jealousy situations and strong possessive love. Thus, in her analysis, we discovered strong feelings of rivalry in relation to her younger sister, who was felt to be the parents', and particularly the father's favourite. In her analysis she recovered both a strong feeling of jealousy and rivalry with her sister for her father's love, and the pervading guilt and depression when her sister died in infancy before the patient was four.

Penis-envy was paramount in her analysis and linked with triangular rivalries; she competed with her father and her older brother for her mother's love. It was also increased by her strong reparative drives in relation to sister-figures, which led to a latent homosexual pattern. Ideas of rivalry with her mother were always the most difficult part of her analysis; though she admired and desired her father, the rivalry with her mother was usually displaced on to sister or brother figures. In the homosexual pattern, on the other hand, the rivalry with her father and brother for her mother was far more freely acknowledged. In the transference, competition for me as a mother-figure overshadowed completely rivalry with me. Eventually, however, some direct oedipal material could be worked through.

At this time I was probably not sufficiently aware of the importance of split-off envy, otherwise I would have been more on the lookout for split-off envious feelings when faced with the patient's resistance to feelings of rivalry in the transference, as well as her marked inhibition in ambition. She could work professionally because of her great interest in the work and its strongly reparative meaning to her, but any awareness of her own ambitious aims would quickly lead to inhibitions in work. Envy came into her analysis quite late, when it seemed that most of her problems were solved. It was heralded by a great deal of disturbance and the appearance of near-psychotic material. First of all, inhibitions in her creative work, which had not troubled her for a long time, re-appeared, accompanied by depression and anxiety. Then gradually there appeared delusional thoughts; she felt that her colleagues, particularly men, were working against her, that her brother had tried to obtain an interview with me to get a vacancy for himself behind her back, that her husband might be unfaithful to her, etc. When these thoughts came to her mind, she knew that they were pure phantasy, but she was disturbed by their delusional nature and the intensity of her irrational feelings. She was frightened by the realization of the fragility of the barrier between sanity and madness. The content of her delusional thoughts was fairly manifest. She was concerned about her rivalry with men and feared their retaliation; she also made reparation to them in phantasy, in giving her husband a better and less frustrating partner, and her brother the good analyst-mother. Gradually the delusional thoughts disappeared, but the patient remained inhibited in her work and unstable in her moods. She felt that her "craziness" had not been fully analysed.

For several months the patient had a small wart on the crown of her head. Though apparently not worried about it, she used to refer to it in her analysis. When disturbed about her own phantasies and irrational feelings, she would complain of having "warts on the brain," and she sometimes associated it with growing a penis, placed in her head and expressed in her intellectual work. One day she reported that she and her husband had been to a party where they received balloons which they brought back to their children. This event she associated with childhood memories of finding balloons or funny hats and paper fans in her room on waking up in the mornings after her parents had been out to carnival balls. These she remembered as wholly happy experiences associated with young, attractive parents and their mysterious and exciting life. The presents they brought her were felt as their attempt to share those things with her.

One thing seemed to have disturbed her at the party. They were with a group of friends, one of whom was an unmarried woman, Joan. She had no dancing partner and left a little before the end of the party. The patient felt unduly worried about Joan not waiting for them, to be given a lift. Joan had occasionally appeared in this patient's analysis; she was a middle-aged spinster suffering from patches of alopecia nervosa. She had been orphaned in early childhood and the patient usually connected her alopecia with this fact.

The next day the patient reported the following dream: She had a growth on her head; it seemed to be a skin disease, but looked very repulsive. It might have been a cancerous growth, though in the dream she was not alarmed, but partly disgusted and partly worried. She particularly noticed that this growth was beside her wart and she seemed surprised. In the dream she had the thought, "And the little wart as well!" as though she expected the growth to have evolved from the wart or to have replaced it, not that she should suffer from both. She showed this growth to her husband as though she wanted to demonstrate something to him. She was not sure whether this was to be a confession or a plea for reassurance or help.

The dream puzzled and disturbed her. She associated the horrible growth on her head with Joan's alopecia. Twice she made a slip and called Joan "Jean." It is a slip she had made occasionally before—Jean being in some way the reverse of Joan, a pretty young woman who had recently had a baby. The appearance of the growth she connected with coloured slides she had seen of the cancer of the womb and of the breast. Yet she persisted in her feeling that it was definitely a skin disease. She connected it also with something like a spoilt balloon losing its air, but dismissed this association. The associations did not seem very meaningful to her but one which carried more feeling than the rest was the association with Joan. She remembered how envious she felt of her sister's pretty hair and Joan appeared to her as her sister returning deprived of everything, without her pretty hair, without parents. Joan having no husband or children represented the fact that her sister never grew up to be a woman since she died in infancy. The patient felt that the illness of her scalp in the dream was an atonement. But though this association brought some relief and understanding, it seemed very incomplete, and suddenly at the end of the session the patient realized that she thought the skin condition was a ringworm, and remembered that a couple of days ago she had heard a Spanish proverb which translates roughly: "If envy were ringworm, how many ringwormy people would there be in the world!" And with that association, she experienced a feeling of enormous relief and understanding; she suddenly felt that everything fell into place.

In the next sessions she realized how envy, like a ring-worm or cancer—the dismissed association representing the dangers that she denied—was the real "wart on her brain" and how it invaded all her relationships and activities. The thought in the dream "The little wart as well!" represented her sudden realization that she was envious and wanted everything for herself; the breast, the womb, the babies, all the feminine achievements, and the penis too. She now realized that, when her parents went to parties, she was in fact consumed with envy. Her relation to her little sister was more complex than it appeared. She not only competed with her for their parents' love, she wished to see her as deprived of everything, not only because she was jealous, but also because she needed a deprived little sister as a vehicle for projection. She wanted her little sister, and not herself, to be suffering from the disfiguring and spoiling envy. The first object of her envy was her mother, represented in her associations by Jean, and it was her balloons—breasts, womb—that she was taking in and spoiling (the spoilt balloon in her associations to the dream). Her mother, as well as her sister, was represented by the deprived Joan, her slip between Jean and Joan indicating the identity of the two. Her envy of the penis was secondary to her envy of her mother. It was partly a displacement from the breast and partly envy of it, not as a masculine attribute, but as yet another desirable possession belonging to the mother. In following sessions she felt that she envied everybody and everything. She envied men their penis and the love of the woman; she envied mothers their new babies; feeding mothers their breasts; married women their husbands; but she also envied the unmarried women their time, free of family or financial worries, and sometimes their greater professional success.

What she had herself, marriage, children, ability and professional success, were spoilt for her by guilt. She felt that they were all connected with the working of her envy. She felt guilty of greed in that indeed she did manage to have both feminine and masculine achievements. But the greatest feeling of guilt was connected with her realization that she was unconsciously using her riches to stimulate envy, just as in the past she had tried to project her envy into her sister.

Her success had to be moderate, as she felt too guilty about having it and too afraid of her projected envy; particularly she could not allow herself creativity in her work, which represented to her competition with her mother for creative, feminine attributes, a competition in which, if successful, she would project overwhelming envy into her mother. Envy was indeed "the wart on her brain," interfering with all creativity. The wart itself dried up and fell off a few days after the analysis of the dream. As envy of myself fully came into the foreground of the analysis, one could see that the spoilt balloons also represented her deflated analysis in which she could allow only a very moderate success, both to me and to herself, as a way of preventing envy in either.

In the material of this patient, one can see how, when envy is successfully split off, the personality can develop relatively well, but at the cost of considerable impoverishment. Moreover, the split-off envy remains a constant source of unconscious guilt and a constant threat that a psychotic part may still break through.

In more normal development, envy becomes more integrated. The gratification experienced at the breast stimulates admiration, love and gratitude at the same time as envy. These feelings enter into conflict as soon as the ego begins to integrate and, if envy is not overwhelming, gratitude overcomes and modifies envy. The ideal breast, introjected with love, gratification and gratitude, becomes part of the ego, the ego is more full of goodness itself. And thus, in a benevolent circle, envy lessens as gratification increases, the diminution of envy allows more gratification which in turn furthers the lessening of envy. Feelings of envy in relation to the primary object, though weakened, always remain. Some of these feelings get displaced from the primary object on to the rival, becoming fused with jealous feelings in relation to the rival. The envy of the mother's breast is displaced on to the father's penis, increasing the rivalry with the father. Such envy as remains in relation to the primary object, when it is no longer felt to be destructively devastating, can become the basis of emulation and rivalry with the primary object, in a way which is egosyntonic and does not give rise to overwhelming feelings of guilt and persecution.

In pathological development, excessive early envy affects fundamentally the course of the paranoid–schizoid position and contributes to its psychopathology.

BIBLIOGRAPHY

MELANIE KLEIN: *Envy and Gratitude.*
HERBERT ROSENFELD: "Some Observations on the Psycho-pathology of Hypochondriacal States," *Int.J.Psycho-Anal.*, vol. 39 (1958).
BETTY JOSEPH: "Some Characteristics of the Psychopathic Personality," *Int.J.Psycho-Anal.*, vol. XLI (1960).

CHAPTER FIVE

THE PSYCHOPATHOLOGY OF THE PARANOID–SCHIZOID POSITION

THE PSYCHOPATHOLOGY of the earliest phase of development is, not surprisingly, the most obscure and difficult problem in psycho-analytical research. It is the phase of development the most remote in time from the actual age at which we see our patients, when their earliest experiences are certain to be modified, distorted and confused with later ones. Furthermore, when observing the behaviour of infants, the younger they are the more difficult it is to interpret. Difficulties encountered in the study of the earliest phases in normal development are very much increased in the presence of pathological phenomena; the more disturbed the infant is, the more remote is his experience from the observing adult's introspective experiences.

Nevertheless, the study of this phase is of paramount importance. We know that the fixation points of psychoses lie in the earliest months of infancy. Furthermore, we know that in psychological illness regression occurs, not to a phase of development that was in itself normal, but to one in which pathological disturbances were present, creating blocks to development and constituting fixation points. We are entitled, therefore, to assume, and our clinical experiences have amply confirmed this assumption, that, in so far as the psychotic regresses to the earliest months of infancy, he regresses to a phase in development which already possessed pathological features in his infancy. Through a study of the case-histories of schizophrenic and schizoid patients, and from observation of infants from birth, we are now increasingly able to diagnose schizoid features in early infancy and foresee future difficulties. The detailed psycho-analysis of schizophrenic patients of all ages, including psychotic children, throws some light on the dynamics of psychological disturbances in early infancy.

I have emphasized in the previous chapter that, in normal development, the paranoid–schizoid position is characterized by a split between the good and the bad objects and the loving and the hating ego, a split in which good experiences predominate over bad ones. This is a necessary pre-condition for integration in later stages of development. I have also emphasized that, at this stage, the infant comes to organize his perceptions by means of projective and introjective processes.

All these processes are disturbed where, for internal or external reasons and most frequently through a combination of both, the bad experience predominates over the good one. It would be far beyond the scope of this chapter to attempt an account of the many pathological changes that may occur in this situation. I shall confine myself to describing a few characteristic pathological phenomena.

Under unfavourable conditions in the paranoid–schizoid position projective identification is used differently from the way it is used in normal development. The features of pathological projective identification were first described by Dr. W. R. Bion.

In normal development, the infant projects part of the self and internal objects into the breast and the mother. These projected parts are relatively unaltered in the process of projection, and when subsequent re-introjection takes place, they can be re-integrated into the ego. Also, these projected parts follow certain psychological and physiological demarcation lines. For instance, the "bad" may be projected, or the "good," or certain organs of perception like sight or hearing, or sexual impulses. The "slippery fox" in the child material presented in the chapter on the paranoid–schizoid position is an example of such a projection.

When anxiety and hostile and envious impulses are intense, however, projective identification happens differently. The

projected part is splintered and disintegrated into minute
fragments, and it is these minute fragments that are projected into the object, disintegrating it in turn into minute
parts. The aim of this violent projective identification is
two-fold. Since, in pathological development, the experience
of reality is felt primarily as a persecution, there is a violent
hatred of all experience of reality, external or internal.
The splintering of the ego is an attempt to get rid of all
perception, and it is the perceptual apparatus that is primarily
attacked, destroyed and obliterated. At the same time, the
object which is responsible for the perception is hated, and
the projection is aimed at destroying that bit of reality—the
hated object—as well as getting rid of the perceptual
apparatus which perceived it. When envy is intense, the
perception of an ideal object is as painful as the experience
of a bad one, since the ideal object arouses unbearable
feelings of envy. Hence, this type of projective identification
may be directed at the ideal object as well as at the persecutory one.

As a consequence of this process of fragmentation there
is no "tidy split" between an ideal and a bad object or objects,
but the object is perceived as being split into minute bits,
each containing a minute and violently hostile part of the
ego. These bits have been described by Bion as "bizarre
objects." The ego itself is severely damaged by this disintegrating process, and its attempts to get rid of the pain
of perception only lead to an increase of painful perceptions,
both through the persecutory nature of the "bizarre objects"
and the painful mutilation of the perceptual apparatus.
Thus a vicious circle is established, in which the painfulness
of reality leads to pathological projective identification, and
this in turn leads to reality becoming increasingly persecutory and painful. That part of reality which is affected
by the process is experienced by the sick infant as filled with
"bizarre objects" charged with enormous hostility, threatening a depleted and mutilated ego.

In my experience, some patients try to save a split-off
part of the object and what remains of the ego by trying to
split off and isolate these "bizarre objects" in a kind of

"third area." For instance, a border-line schizoid patient said "I can't get in touch with you. Here is my head on the pillow and there are you in your armchair. But between the top of my head and you there is nothing but horrible bloody mish-mash." On further analysis, we understood that this "bloody mish-mash" was associated with his experience of feeding from a breast where a breast abscess was forming. The "mish-mash" was perceived by him as bitten-up, pussy particles of the breast, containing the patient's own urine, faeces and broken-off bits of his teeth. He could preserve something of his "head," standing for his sanity, and a remote analyst in the armchair, but there was no relation between him and myself. The real relationship between his mouth and the breast was happening in the "third area," in the "mish-mash" split off both from the analyst-mother and the patient-infant.

Similarly, a hebephrenic adolescent patient of mine paid no attention to me but was wholly preoccupied by the pillow on the analytic couch. It appeared on analysis that the pillow represented the breast containing the patient's projected infant head. Interpretations about the pillow standing for the breast had no meaning for her, but when I interpretated that the pillow stood for the breast containing the head and that she was splitting off this head–breast relationship from the relationship between herself and her mother, a marked change occurred in the transference. The patient became aware of me and experienced an overtly hostile and persecutory transference. Whenever the transference became too intense, she would again split off the "third area" and become uniquely concerned with the pillow and sometimes with other trappings of the couch.

The attack on reality by projective identification is connected with another process characteristic of the paranoid–schizoid position, also described by Bion, namely the attacks on linking: any function or organ that is perceived by the infant to link objects together is violently attacked. Thus the infant's own mouth and the nipple get destroyed since they are a link between the infant and the breast. As in the patient whom I have quoted above, instead of a link between patient and analyst, the baby and the mother, his attacks produced a "bloody mish-mash." Similarly, the hebephrenic adolescent had a habit of tearing threads out of the pillow and the couch, and then tearing them into tiny fragments. In insightful moments, she acknowledged that she was trying to break her links with the external world, her "chains" as she called them. In this way, links are attacked and broken between the self and the object, internal and external, and various parts of the self, e.g. the link between the functions of feeling and thinking. Links between other objects become in turn the objects of tremendously envious attacks, since the infant feels himself incapable of linking and is particularly envious of the capacity in others of linking together. Of course, the more he attacks the links between the objects he internalizes, the less is he capable of linking and the more envious he becomes.

These links perceived between objects are immediately sexualized and many analysts dealing with schizophrenics are convinced that a schizoid infant has prematurely genital phantasies and experiences, premature violent sexual envy and jealousy. The Oedipus complex then remains at an oral level and is characterized not by jealousy but by intense envy of the parental relationship.

The schizoid infant lives in a world very different from that of a normal child. His perceptual apparatus is damaged, he feels himself surrounded by disintegrated hostile objects, his links with reality are either broken or very painful and his capacity to link and to integrate is disrupted. In order to survive under such conditions, the infant must try by some means or other to preserve a part of the ego capable of feeding and to establish an object sufficiently good, in relation to which feeding and other introjective processes such as learning can be achieved. He is faced with the task of splitting off and maintaining an ideal object protected from the devastating effects of his projective identification. I should like to give here an example of one such attempt.

The patient who complained of the "mish-mash" went through a phase of acute persecutory feelings in relation to his wife. In particular, he suspected her of intentionally spoiling his food and, upon occasion, of actually poisoning it. He also suspected her of being dangerously ambivalent and even murderous towards their baby. He frequently accused me of siding with his wife, and gradually his suspicions were more fully brought into the transference. At the same time, the patient idealized himself, particularly his relationship with his baby and his work. When some of this material had been worked through, and in particular when his self-idealization and the projection of bad parts of himself had been partly analysed, he recognized clearly and feelingly his own previous attacks on the analysis, representing both the mother's food and her creation—the baby.

Following a particularly convincing insight, he came to a session in a very different mood. His baby had been unwell in the night and he heard her cry, but he did not get up. He contrasted his behaviour with his wife's immediate readiness to attend to their baby, her generous love and care, and her patience in dealing both with the baby and himself. He also commented on my patience in dealing with his various accusations and projections. He added, however, in a mocking voice, "Since, whenever I said bad things about my wife, you interpreted that they were bad parts of myself which I put into her, I suppose now, when I say such good things about her, and about yourself, you will interpret that these are good parts of myself, which I only see in others." Though his association was derisive, I interpreted that this was indeed what he felt. I suggested that he had to project these good parts because, if he retained them inside himself, he would expose himself to conflict and work. If he retained the love for his baby, he would have to get up at night to care for her. If he retained his love for the analysis he would have to care for it inside himself and protect it from his own bad impulses.

As soon as the patient became aware of his own destructiveness, he had to project his good part outside lest it should be overwhelmed by the bad part in an inner conflict. Thus, he established his wife and myself, standing for his mother, as the ideal objects containing all the good parts of himself, leaving him wholly bad and depleted. This configuration corresponded with many situations in which the patient left all the work that had to be done to me in the transference or to his wife at home. This idealization, however, was very precarious. Halfway through the session the patient remembered with fury that he had made over to his wife his best financial shares and he hated her for it. He felt robbed and depleted. This was followed by a complaint that the analysis robbed him of his self-esteem and made him feel valueless. His ideal object was immediately felt also as a persecutor. He could not tolerate the effects of his own idealization. From the moment that he gave over to his ideal object his "best shares," he felt that it had stolen his goodness. At the same time, his envy was enormously increased, so that the ideal object again became the focus for attacks and hostile projections.

Here is another illustration of the complex difficulties involved in maintaining an ideal object when pathological paranoid–schizoid processes are prevalent. The patient, a middle-aged woman, was going through a phase of acute hypochondriasis with manic, paranoid and depressive features. She believed herself to be suffering from a germ infection of a generalized kind, which she felt was responsible for her instability of mood and general exhaustion. She described luridly and vividly how the germs attacked her central nervous system, interfering with her thinking and her suprarenal glands and exhausting her; how they invaded her sense-organs, causing hyperacuity of hearing and sight. There was no doubt that her internal persecutors were of the "bizarre objects" kind. They were split off from people with whom the patient tried to maintain a relation free of persecution.

The people with whom she had relationships were divided into two categories. The people in the first category were felt to be dependent on her. She felt responsible for them, concerned about them and guilty if she neglected them. They were all felt to be on the verge of a mental "breakdown." These people were containers of her own projected "breakdown." The people in the second category were fewer: she intensely idealized her husband and one or two other men, and depended upon them, though the dependence was strenuously denied. It soon appeared, however, that the split was not successfully maintained. One after another of her ideal objects was suspected of having "a breakdown." Urine had always played a predominant part in her analysis. In this context, her urine was felt as resulting from such minute disintegration of her internal objects and parts of herself that all shape was lost; it was experienced as a stream of germs which she poured into her object. Her speech, which was manic, flooding, demanding and intruding, was felt and used as a stream of urine with which she could project her "breakdown" into her object.

For a while the patient was very resistant to transference interpretations, until one day she reported that she had had a dream. It was about a chamber-pot which could not be used because it was covered with a chintz cover—a situation which, in the dream, threw her into a state of despair and rage. She associated this dream with the fact that the previous afternoon she had rung me up about a change of session and thought me short and brusque on the phone.

The work done following this dream illuminated the patient's relation to me as an ideal object. Her ideal object at this time was a chamber-pot—a breast into which she could pour her urine, the object that could contain her "breakdown" without breaking down. If I appeared to be unaffected by the patient's projections, she experienced me as blocking her projective identification and as being as useless as a chamber-pot covered with a lid; she was then left bursting with germs and urine. If, however, I appeared in any way affected by the patient's projections, for instance looking paler or having a slight cold, the patient felt that all "the breakdown" was projected into me, which at first made me an object of some concern; but very soon I turned into a persecutor, pouring disintegration and germs back into her. On rare occasions, when the patient gained insight into the whole process, she could feel me as the ideal object fulfilling her demand, taking in her "breakdown" and tolerating it without actually breaking down and becoming vengeful. Such an experience brought temporary relief, but increased her envy and her frantic urinary attacks. The recognition of her relation to her original ideal object, expressed in the dream in which the pot stood for the analyst—the breast-pot, was so intolerable that she had to split it into three types of relation that preoccupied her: her germs (sheer persecution), her ideal objects and her objects of concern (mixture of depression and persecution). This splitting of her object defended her against the realization that it was her own attacks which converted her ideal object into the urine-germs; and that it was her use of this infected urine to attack the external object which brought about the breakdown of her ideal object.

To illustrate more fully some pathological processes, I shall give an almost complete account of a first session with an adolescent schizophrenic girl. For the sake of clarity, I shall divide the session into several sequences.

The patient was a girl of sixteen, with a long history of schizophrenic illness. She came to London, from a little town, X, soon after her father had committed suicide. The patient was not told that it was a suicide and was supposed not to know. When her mother told her about the arrangements for her treatment she asked only one question: Was the analyst married and did she have children?

First Sequence: She came in, looked around, skipped a few times round the room and immediately began talking. She said that she came to treatment because she could not concentrate on work, but she did not think that she was going to do much talking because she knew that I expected her to talk, and when people wanted her to talk, she wanted to be silent. She only wanted to talk when she thought others wanted her to be silent. Anyway, talking was pointless. People always talked about health and marriages and having children and nothing else. She had not got either, so she did not have any interest in these topics. Then the patient looked around again and muttered under her breath "I can only talk about sickness and that makes everyone around me sick." Then in a louder voice she said "People talk a lot about sickness and that is no good to me, it only makes me sick. Anyway, all my family did nothing but quarrel and talk about sickness."

In the first sequence, the patient shows a sudden change of perception. At the beginning "people always talk about health and marriages and having children," and at the end they do "nothing but quarrel or talk about sickness." Underlying this change of perception there is a dynamic process. She sees in me a healthy married person with children, which repeats her experience of her parents as a married couple. Compared with me—her parents—she feels that she contains nothing but sickness. She envies me, as she envied her parents their healthy married state, and she feels that through talking she can project illness into them ("I only talk sickness and it makes everybody sick"), so that, in the process of her talking, she makes her family quarrel and be sick. Then they in turn invade her with the sickness. The feeling of envy for her parents and her analyst is unconscious and she is only dimly conscious of the nature of her attacks. What she is aware of, however, is the danger of talking.*

Second Sequence: After my interpretation, pointing out to her her attack and fear of retaliation, the patient said that anyway she saw in people "nothing but projections of characters in books." She described how she liked reading books, devouring books. The characters in a book, she said, were to her far more real than any other people, and yet they were so unreal. Characters in books could have all the emotions; she herself lacked them. Characters in books were wonderful because she could do with them whatever she pleased. She did not even mind hurting them because they never changed.

In the second sequence the patient shows the split that exists in her mind. The real people around her, she feels, are made sick by her projections and become persecutors who in turn project into her and make her sick. She therefore puts all her love into characters in a book and these

---

* The work with this patient was done before the publication of *Envy and Gratitude* and it is interesting to note how, in the analysis of the psychotic, unconscious envy immediately comes to the fore.

become her ideal objects. But when she has projected all her sickness—badness—into the real people and all her love and ideal qualities into the characters in a book, the patient herself feels completely depleted. She has no emotions or contents, either good or bad. In order to counteract this, she has to devour books in an attempt to get these ideal objects inside herself and to get back the projected parts of herself which are now in them. She also gives a hint as to why characters in a book, rather than real people, become her ideal objects. They fulfil better her conditions for an ideal object. It has not only to be perfect and indestructible, but also completely compliant. ("I can do with them whatever I please.")

Third Sequence: I made a brief interpretation, pointing out the split and the idealization, and in doing so used an expression "and now you have to take those book characters inside you." On hearing the word "inside," the patient showed a sudden change of behaviour. She showed unmistakable signs of experiencing some violent internal persecution. She wrung her hands, doubled up her body, moaned and muttered under her breath, so that I could only catch the words "inside," "pains," "body sensation," "pain in the nail." I interpreted her fear of words getting inside her, controlling her and giving her pain. Without responding, she began a new trend of associations.

Fourth Sequence: She started talking in an animated fashion about her past—about being in a boarding school from the age of four and how wonderful it was. "It did not matter what you did and whom you did it to." Then she said that she and Mummy left Daddy when she herself was two.* They collected all the sick people on the railway and on the road and got evacuated with them. At four she decided to go to boarding school and left both her parents.

In response to my comment about leaving her father behind, she said "Oh, it did not matter in the least. I didn't know one person from another." She then started

---

* She was in fact evacuated with her mother at the age of two and when she was four she was left as a boarder in the school she attended then, apparently at her own insistent request.

looking round the room very anxiously. I suggested that she was now looking for her father and it might be that she missed him as she had missed him when she was two. She laughed and said "Missing Daddy now—in London? That couldn't be, not here! People are not missed where they never were. If I were in X, maybe I would have felt something about him, but I couldn't feel about him in London, when I left him in X." I interpreted that she felt she had left part of herself behind and cut herself off from her own memories, leaving them in X, and she said very loudly "Oh, yes. Except that things follow you around, worms, caterpillars, things in dreams and skeletons jumping out of cupboards."*

In this sequence the patient shows a reintrojection of the projected sickness. Her father, whom she left behind, becomes split in her mind into thousands of sick people, whom she feels she at first has to take inside and then to "evacuate." She also shows some of the mechanisms of defence against guilt and persecution, resulting from the destruction of her object—her father. For instance, she splits herself in space and time, leaving a part of herself in any place as she leaves it. The father, who died in X, and the part of herself that introjected him, are cut off, left in X, and momentarily she believes them to be omnipotently annihilated. Immediately, however, she confesses the failure of this mechanism; she feels that this destroyed object, split into little bits, as well as the part of herself that she tried to leave behind, follows her around in the shape of worms, caterpillars, etc.

The next part of the session was concerned with her relationship to her younger sister, and I shall not report it here as it follows a pattern very similar to that of her relation to the father. Towards the end of the session, she gave a clear description of her internal world.

Fifth Sequence: "It is rather like the man in the Bible. He lived in a wonderful castle in which he collected all sorts of treasures, but this castle was overrun by horrid creatures and vermin, and he was exiled into a little cottage." When

---

* This unconscious reference to her father's suicide is typical of schizophrenic thinking.

I interpreted that this was what she felt about herself and that it was in her internal world that she was exiled from the castle and had to live in a little cottage, she said very sadly, and looking sane for the first time in the session, "Yes, but he shouldn't have done it, not in that way in the first place."

In this last sequence the patient shows very clearly her feelings about her internal world. She feels split, there is a part of herself like the castle, full of richness, her ideal objects and their wonderful qualities, and another part poor and verminous. She feels that she has taken in the good things greedily and enviously and in so doing she feels that she has deprived people of all goodness. They have become empty and bad and turned into vermin that persecute her. She feels invaded by the vermin (the sickness at the beginning of the session) and is exiled from the castle of her dreams, and in her internal world she has to live in a split-off depleted part of herself—the little cottage—devoid of feeling, sensation, and any experience except that of poverty and persecution.

BIBLIOGRAPHY

W. BION: *Second Thoughts* (Heinemann Medical Books, 1967).
H. ROSENFELD: "Notes on the Psycho-analysis of the Super-ego Conflict of an Acute Schizophrenic Patient," *Int.J.Psycho-Anal.*, vol. 33 (1952). *New Directions in Psycho-analysis* (Chapter 8).
HANNA SEGAL: "Depression in the Schizophrenic," *Int.J.Psycho-Anal.*, vol. 37 (1956).

CHAPTER SIX

THE DEPRESSIVE POSITION

IN DESCRIBING the paranoid–schizoid position, I tried to show how a successful negotiation of the anxieties experienced in the early months of the infant's development leads to a gradual organization of his universe. As the processes of splitting, projection and introjection help to sort out his perceptions and emotions and divide the good from the bad, the infant feels himself to be confronted with an ideal object, which he loves and tries to acquire, keep and identify with, and a bad object, into which he has projected his aggressive impulses and which is felt to be a threat to himself and his ideal object.

If the conditions of development are favourable, the infant will increasingly feel that his ideal object and his own libidinal impulses are stronger than the bad object and his bad impulses; he will be able more and more to identify with his ideal object and, because of this identification, as well as because of the physiological growth and development of his ego, he will feel increasingly that his ego is becoming stronger and better able to defend itself and its ideal object. When the infant feels that his ego is strong and securely possessed of a strong ideal object, he will be less frightened of his own bad impulses and therefore less driven to project them outside. When the projection of bad impulses decreases, the power attributed to the bad object will decrease too, while the ego will become stronger as it is less impoverished by projection. The infant's tolerance of the death instinct within himself increases and his paranoid fears lessen; splitting and projection decrease and the drive towards integration of the ego and the object can gradually take the upper hand.

From the start, there is a tendency towards integration, as well as towards splitting, and throughout the infant's development, even in the earliest months, he will experience moments of more or less complete integration. But when the integrative processes become more stable and continual, a new phase of development is engendered—the depressive position.

The depressive position has been defined by Melanie Klein as that phase of development in which the infant recognizes a whole object and relates himself to this object. This is a crucial moment in the infant's development, and one which is clearly recognized by laymen. Everyone who surrounds him will perceive a change and recognize it as an enormous step in his development—they will notice and comment on the fact that the infant now recognizes his mother. Soon after, as we know, he rapidly begins to recognize other people in his environment, first, usually, his father. When the infant recognizes his mother, it means that now he perceives her as a whole object. When we speak of the infant recognizing his mother as a whole object, we contrast this with both part-object relationships and split-object relationships; the infant, that is to say, relates himself more and more, not only to the mother's breast, hands, face, eyes, as separate objects, but to herself as a whole person, who can be at times good, at times bad, present or absent, and who can be both loved and hated. He begins to see that his good and bad experiences do not proceed from a good and a bad breast or mother, but from the same mother who is the source of good and bad alike. This recognition of his mother as a whole person has very wide implications, and opens up a world of new experience. Recognizing his mother as a whole person means also recognizing her as an individual who leads a life of her own and has relationships with other people. The infant discovers his helplessness, his utter dependence on her, and his jealousy of other people.

Together with this altered perception of the object, there is a fundamental change in the ego because, as the mother becomes a whole object, so the infant's ego becomes a whole ego and is less and less split into its good and bad components. The integration of both ego and object proceed simultaneously. The lessening of projective processes and the greater integration of the ego means that the perception of objects is less distorted so that the bad and ideal objects are brought closer together. At the same time, introjection of an increasingly whole object promotes integration in the ego. These psychological changes help along, and are helped by, physiological maturation in the ego, the maturation of the central nervous system allowing a better organization of perceptions arising in different physiological areas and allowing for the development and organization of memory. When the mother is perceived as a whole object, the infant is better able to remember her, that is, to remember former gratification at times when she seems to be depriving him and former experiences of deprivation when she is gratifying him. As these processes of integration proceed, the infant realizes more and more clearly that it is the same person— himself—who loves and hates the same person—his mother. He is then faced with conflicts pertaining to his own ambivalence. This change in the state of ego- and object-integration brings with it a change in the focus of the infant's anxieties. In the paranoid–schizoid position, the main anxiety is that the ego will be destroyed by the bad object or objects. In the depressive position, anxieties spring from ambivalence, and the child's main anxiety is that his own destructive impulses have destroyed or will destroy, the object that he loves and totally depends on.

In the depressive position, introjective processes are intensified. This is partly due to the lessening of projective mechanisms and partly to the infant's discovery of his dependence on his object which he now perceives as independent and liable to go away. This increases his need to possess this object, keep it inside and, if possible, to protect it from his own destructiveness. The depressive position begins in the oral phase of development, when love and need lead to devouring. The omnipotence of oral introjective mechanisms leads to anxiety lest powerful destructive impulses destroy not only the good external object, but the good introjected object as well. This good internal object forms the core of the ego and the infant's internal world, so that the infant feels himself faced with anxiety lest he destroy his whole internal world.

The more integrated infant who can remember and retain love for the good object even while hating it, will be exposed to new feelings little known in the paranoid–schizoid position: the mourning and pining for the good object felt as lost and destroyed, and guilt, a characteristic depressive experience which arises from the sense that he has lost the good object through his own destructiveness. At the height of his ambivalence he is exposed to depressive despair. He remembers that he has loved, and indeed still loves his mother, but feels that he has devoured or destroyed her so that she is no longer available in the external world. Furthermore, he has also destroyed her as an internal object, which is now felt to be in bits. The infant's internal world is felt to be in bits in identification with this object and acute feelings of loss are experienced, as well as guilt, pining and hopelessness about regaining it. To this suffering on his own behalf is added suffering on behalf of his mother, because of the undying love he has for her and the constant intro-jection and identification with her. His pains are further increased by feelings of persecution, partly because, at the height of depressive feelings, some regression will recur, in which bad feelings will again be projected and identified with internal persecutors, and partly because the good object in bits, which stimulates such intense feelings of loss and guilt, is again experienced to some extent as a persecutor.

Here is a typical dream, dreamt by a patient who felt herself threatened by an experience of depressive despair. She was a manic-depressive patient, and at the time of the dream she was in an interval fairly free from either depression or mania. On the day preceding the dream, it had become clear that the continuation of her analysis was threatened through financial difficulties, and she had asked me whether I would continue the treatment if she were unable to pay her fees for a time. As her difficulties in the external world seemed very real, I gave her some indication that I did not consider ending her treatment at that point.

The next day the patient opened the session by complaining that my waiting-room was very cold. She also thought, for the first time, that it looked very drab and dreary, and she deplored the lack of curtains in the room. Following these associations, she reported a dream. She said that the dream was very simple—she had just dreamt of a sea of icebergs; they were coming in unending waves, so that you could not see the sea, the blue sea itself, but only these enormous white mountains coming in great waves, one after another. In the dream she was acutely aware that these icebergs went very deep indeed and that the white, cold mountains that she saw on the surface of the sea were only a fragment of the mountainous ice beneath the surface. She said that on waking her first thought was that she was afraid she might soon be in the grip of depression again. The dream, she said, showed more clearly than any previous one what her depression really felt like—it was like being in the grip of those icebergs, which filled her so that nothing of her personality was left—she herself was turned into an iceberg with no feelings and no warmth left in her. She then associated with the icebergs a poem about ancient and deserted ships, looking like swans asleep. They also reminded her of the white and wavy hair of an old friend of hers, Mrs. A., who used to be kind to her, from whom she had had help and whom she had neglected, which caused her a great deal of guilt and sorrow.

After these associations, I interpreted that the cold waiting-room was the same as the cold icebergs in her dream; that she must feel that her demands to pay reduced fees or no fees at all had completely exhausted and impoverished me—the waiting-room being drab and dreary and without curtains—that she had in fact killed me, so that I had become like a cold iceberg, filling her with guilt and persecution.

She then added a few more associations. She suddenly realized that those wild waves were breast-shaped, she thought that they were like dead or frozen breasts, and also that the jagged edges were like teeth. Furthermore, she told me that the preceding night she had met Mrs. A at a party; she had wanted to hand Mrs. A a cup of tea, but Mrs. A had said "No, thank you," she preferred coffee. It was at that moment that the patient felt that she experienced for the first time that day a slight premonition of recurring depression. She thought that Mrs. A looked cold and disapproving, and then she comforted herself with the thought that maybe Mrs. A looked sad simply because her son-in-law had died recently.

These associations elucidate the dream further. To begin with, they make it clear that the patient's demand on me in financial terms was unconsciously experienced by her as a greedy, biting and devouring attack on my breasts. Furthermore, she makes it clear that it is her feeling of incapacity to restore me (represented by Mrs. A) after this attack, that really brings out the feeling of depression. She makes an attempt at reparation, offering Mrs. A a cup of tea, but her reparation is refused—Mrs. A prefers coffee. From other material in this patient's analysis, it was quite clear to us that she felt that Mrs. A had refused her cup of tea because she, the patient, was a woman. She wanted a cup of coffee from her son-in-law, standing for the patient's brother. Since the patient is not a man, she feels that she cannot make reparation to the breast, and at that moment her wish to make reparation, and even her sorrow disappear, and Mrs. A is perceived as a persecutor: she is cold and she is disapproving. In the dream, this element of persecution is represented by the iceberg-breasts having teeth. After the way in which the patient feels that she has emptied the breast and bitten it, she now experiences the feeling of an empty, cold, dead and biting breast filling her completely and destroying her own ego, which, in the dream, is the blue sea that cannot be seen.

The experience of depression mobilizes in the infant the wish to repair his destroyed object or objects. He longs to make good the damage inflicted in his omnipotent phantasy, to restore and regain his lost loved objects, and to give them back life and wholeness. Believing that his own destructive attacks have been responsible for the destruction of the object, he also believes that his own love and care can undo the effects of his aggression. The depressive conflict is a constant struggle between the infant's destructiveness and his love and reparative impulses. Failure of reparation leads to despair, its success to renewed hope. More will be said about the conditions for reparation later on. Suffice it here to say that the gradual resolution of depressive anxieties and the regaining of good objects externally and internally can be achieved by the reparation made by the infant, in reality and in omnipotent phantasy, to his external and internal objects.

The depressive position marks a crucial step in the infant's development, and its working through is accompanied by a radical alteration in his view of reality. When the ego becomes more integrated, when the processes of projection lessen and when the infant begins to perceive his dependence on an external object and the ambivalence of his own instincts and aims, he discovers his own psychic reality. The infant becomes aware of himself and of his objects as separate from himself. He becomes aware of his own impulses and phantasies, and begins to distinguish between phantasy and external reality. The development of his sense of psychic reality is inseparably bound up with his growing sense of external reality, and he begins to differentiate between the two.

Reality testing exists from birth. The child "tastes" his experiences, and classifies them as good or bad. But in the depressive position this reality testing becomes more established and meaningful and more closely connected with psychic reality. When the infant becomes more fully aware of his own impulses, good and bad, they are felt by him to be omnipotent, but concern for his object makes him follow closely the impact on it of his impulses and actions, and he gradually tests out the power of his impulses and his object's resilience. In favourable circumstances, the mother's reappearance after absence, her care and attention, gradually modify the infant's belief in the omnipotence of his destructive impulses. The failure of his magical reparation similarly diminishes his belief in the omnipotence of his love. He gradually discovers the limits of both his hate and his love, and with the growth and development of his ego he discovers more and more actual ways of affecting external reality.

At the same time, right through the development and the working through of the depressive position, there is a strengthening of the ego, by growth and by the assimilation of good objects, which are introjected into the ego and also into the superego.

Once this step in development has been achieved, the infant's relation to reality has been established. The fixation point of the psychotic illnesses lies in the paranoid–schizoid position and at the beginning of the depressive position. When regression occurs to these early points in development, the sense of reality is lost and the individual becomes psychotic. If the depressive position has been reached and at least partially worked through, the difficulties encountered in the later development of the individual are not of a psychotic, but of a neurotic nature.

The whole relationship to objects alters as the depressive position is gradually worked through. The infant acquires the capacity to love and respect people as separate, differentiated individuals. He becomes capable of acknowledging his impulses, of feeling a sense of responsibility for them and of tolerating guilt. The new capacity to feel concern for his objects helps him to learn gradually to control his impulses.

The character of the super-ego changes. The ideal and the persecutory objects which were introjected in the paranoid–schizoid position form the first roots of the super-ego. The persecutory object is experienced as punitive in a retaliatory, ruthless fashion. The ideal object with which the ego longs to identify becomes the ego-ideal part of the super-ego, often also persecuting because of the high demands for perfection.

As the ideal and persecutory objects come together in the depressive position, the super-ego becomes more integrated and is experienced as an internal whole, ambivalently loved object. Injury to this object give rise to feelings of guilt and self-reproach. In the early phases of the depressive position the super-ego is still felt as very severe and persecuting (the iceberg with teeth in the dream of the severely depressed patient), but as the whole object relation is more fully established the super-ego loses some of its monstrous aspects and approximates more to the view of good and loved parents. Such a super-ego is not only the source of guilt but also an object of love and one felt by the child as helpful in his struggle against his destructive impulses.

The pain of mourning experienced in the depressive position, and the reparative drives developed to restore the loved internal and external objects, are the basis of creativity and sublimation. These reparative activities are directed towards both the object and the self. They are done partly because of concern for and guilt towards the object, and the wish to restore, preserve and give it eternal life; and partly in the interest of self-preservation, now more realistically orientated. The infant's longing to recreate his lost objects gives him the impulse to put together what has been torn asunder, to reconstruct what has been destroyed, to recreate and to create. At the same time, his wish to spare his objects leads him to sublimate his impulses when they are felt to be destructive. Thus, his concern for his object modifies his instinctual aims and brings about an inhibition of instinctual drives. And as the ego becomes better organized and projections are weakened, repression takes over from splitting. Psychotic mechanisms gradually give way to neurotic mechanisms, inhibition, repression and displacement.

At this point the genesis of symbol formation can be seen. In order to spare the object, the infant partly inhibits his instincts and partly displaces them on to substitutes—the beginning of symbol formation. The processes of sublimation and symbol formation are closely linked and are both the outcome of conflicts and anxieties pertaining to the depressive position.

One of Freud's greatest contributions to psychology was the discovery that sublimation is the outcome of a successful renunciation of an instinctual aim; I would like to suggest here that such a successful renunciation can only happen

through a process of mourning. The giving up of an instinctual aim, or object, is a repetition and at the same time a re-
living of the giving up of the breast. It can be successful, like
this first situation, if the object to be given up can be assimilated
in the ego, by the process of loss and internal restoration.
I suggest that such an assimilated object becomes a symbol
within the ego. Every aspect of the object, every situation
that has to be given up in the process of growing, gives rise
to symbol formation.

In this view symbol formation is the outcome of a loss, it is
a creative work involving the pain and the whole work of
mourning.

If psychic reality is experienced and differentiated from
external reality, the symbol is differentiated from the object;*
it is felt to be created by the self and can be freely used by
the self.†

In the depressive position, then, the whole climate of
thought changes. It is at this time that the capacities for
linking and abstraction develop, and form the basis of the
kind of thinking we look for in the mature ego, in contrast
to the disjointed and concrete thinking characteristic of the
paranoid–schizoid position.

As the infant goes through repeated experiences of mourning and reparation, loss and recovery, his ego becomes
enriched by the objects which he has had to recreate within
himself and which become part of him. His confidence in
his capacity to retain or recover good objects increases, as
well as his belief in his own love and potentialities.

I should like to illustrate various aspects of integration
which occur in the depressive position with the following
material taken from the analysis of a little girl of four. The
two sessions, parts of which I want to describe, happened
on the eve of an Easter holiday which coincided with Ann's
birthday. This holiday was in some ways particularly
traumatic to Ann, since, the previous holiday, there had been

---

* This is in contrast with "symbolic equation" in which the symbol is
equated with the original object, giving rise to concrete thinking. *Vide* "Notes
on Symbol Formation," *International Journal of Psychoanalysis, 1957.*

† H. Segal. "A Psychoanalytic Contribution to Aesthetics," *International
Journal of Psychoanalysis,* 1952.

an unusually long break in her treatment. She had experienced these two holidays primarily in terms of birth
phantasies and early oral deprivation.

Some time before Easter she started coming to sessions
carrying a soft white cushion against her chest and sucking
her thumb. The sessions were mainly concerned with her
doubt as to whether her mother ever breast-fed her or gave
her a bottle from the start, keeping all the breast to herself.
(In fact, Ann was bottle-fed from birth.) About a fortnight
before the holiday, she developed a severe cold and had to
miss a few sessions. When she returned, it was clear that
she felt that she had killed and destroyed me, standing for
the bad mother who had deprived her of the breast, and that
her cold was felt by her as containing a bad and poisonous
breast that was damaging her in retaliation. She tried to
deal with this situation by total reversal. When she came
back after her cold, I had to be an ill child in bed and she
was the feeding mother, but as a feeding mother she treated
me badly, not feeding me when I was hungry, continually
leaving me while she went "out to a show," and showering
me with presents which I was supposed not really to want
as they were no substitute either for her presence or her food.
She was also extremely controlling and soon it appeared
that she had to control me because she felt that, as a baby
dependent on her and feeling deprived by her, I could only
hate her. In spite of playing the rôle of mother, she often
sucked her thumb and clung to the pillow, which she would
take with her even when she was "going to a show." I was
able to show her that she identified with a mother whom
she envied because mother had all the breast to herself
to enjoy at all times, and also how, in spite of her possession
of the breast which enabled her to push me into the position
of the deprived baby, she still felt very infantile herself, as
she could only use the breast as a baby would, sucking it
and enjoying it.

She was defending herself against depressive anxiety, due
to the coming separation and to her attack on the internal
breast, by reversal and projective identification. She projected the baby part of herself into me, while she magically

identified with me—mother—by introjection. This lasted several days until, towards the end of a session four days before the holiday, she asked me to make a round watch for her. It was the first time since her cold that she had in any way admitted my grown-upness and sought my help. When I had made a watch out of paper, she asked me to attach a long string to it. I asked her what time the hands were to show and she answered without hesitation "seven o'clock." When asked why, she said it was "getting-up time." She was not allowed to go to her parent's bedroom before seven o'clock in the morning.

I interpreted the watch as mainly representing her reality sense; essentially she felt that I was the mother with the round breast represented by the watch and that she herself was the baby. I also interpreted that my holiday was felt by her as the long night during which she had to be alone, while I—or mother—was away with father. But seven o'clock represented getting-up time, standing for her hope of coming back to her treatment after the holiday. If she owned a watch—a reality sense—it meant that she must experience the long night—holiday—and control her impulses to interrupt it; but on the other hand it helped to know that I would come back and that she would regain me as she regained her mother every morning at seven.

She started the next session by again putting me to bed as a sick little girl, but immediately asked me to get up and to make another watch. She asked me to paint it pale blue and to put a string on it. She also asked me if she would be allowed to take it home with her. I had not taken up the significance of the string in the previous session; now I interpreted her wish to take inside herself a breast represented by all the treatment she felt she had had and interpreted the string as her wish to keep in touch with me through this good internalization. The patient then asked me to make another watch exactly the same, but to paint it yellow and not to put a string on it. Then she contemplated both watches for a long time. When I pointed out to her the similarity and the difference in colour, she said they were two "same breasts" but "filled with something else." One was filled

with "colourfulness" and the other filled with "wee-wee."
(Splitting.)

As she had previously spilt a glass of water on the couch
when she put me to bed on it, I interpreted that one watch
was Mummy's breast full of milk, while the other was
Mummy's breast when she felt that she had angrily filled
it with wee-wee. I also said that she did not want a string
on the yellow one because she did not want to take the bad
"wee-wee" breast inside her. She then, with a roguish smile,
produced the watch which I had made for her the day
before and showed me that she had cut big holes in it with
a pair of scissors. So now there were three breasts, a good
one full of milk, a bad one full of wee-wee, and an inter-
mediate one which had been good the day before, but which
she showed me she herself had cut, and therefore spoiled.
I interpreted to her that another reason why she did not
want the string attached to the bad yellow breast was
because she did not want to see the link between her own
angry activities, biting and urinating in anger, and the
breast turning bad. She then took the blue and yellow
watches, connected them with the string, and hung them
on the knobs of two small top drawers in the chest of drawers,
and contemplated them with great satisfaction. I interpreted
to her how the good and bad breast had become integrated
through her discovery of her own ambivalence. At that
she became interested in the bottom drawer of the chest,
tried a key in the keyhole and said "I can't have this one,
can I?" I interpreted to her that now the top drawers
represented Mummy's breasts and the bottom drawer her
genital, which she felt she couldn't have because it was
Daddy's and only his key—penis—fitted into it. I told her
that she saw in me not just a breast, either good or bad, but
a whole person whose breasts seemed good or bad according
to what she felt about me and what she thought she did to
me. She saw me as a person with a whole body and a genital
relationship to Daddy, to which she had no access.

The striking thing in this material is how closely connected
the various aspects of integration were and how this integration was accompanied by progress in her reality sense. The

interpretation of her projective identification enabled the child to regain the deprived baby part of herself. In becoming a baby again, she re-experienced the splitting of the breast (the yellow and blue watches). My interpretation of the splitting made her aware of her own aggression and the breast became integrated (the three watches connected by the string). The integration of the good and bad breast was immediately followed, by the part-object relation becoming a whole-object relation, not only in terms of the contrast between good and bad, but also in terms of the contrast between part- and whole-object, setting the stage for the Oedipus complex. Concurrently with that, and dependent on it, was the child's realization of her own ambivalence and her omnipotent phantasies. At the same time, however, her belief in the omnipotence of those phantasies was modified through reality testing, which enabled her to preserve the idea of me realistically as a person who would go away on holiday and return unchanged at the appointed time.

The depressive position is never fully worked through. The anxieties pertaining to ambivalence and guilt, as well as situations of loss, which reawaken depressive experiences, are always with us. Good external objects in adult life always symbolize and contain aspects of the primary good object, internal and external, so that any loss in later life re-awakens the anxiety of losing the good internal object and, with this anxiety, all the anxieties experienced originally in the depressive position. If the infant has been able to establish a good internal object relatively securely in the depressive position, situations of depressive anxiety will not lead to illness, but to a fruitful working through, leading to further enrichment and creativity.

Where the depressive position has not been worked through sufficiently, and the belief in the ego's love and creativity and its capacity to regain good objects internally and externally has not been firmly established, development is far less favourable. The ego is dogged by constant anxiety of the total loss of good internal situations, it is impoverished and weakened, its relation to reality may be tenuous and there is a perpetual dread of and sometimes an actual threat of regression into psychosis.

BIBLIOGRAPHY

MELANIE KLEIN: "Contribution to the Psycho-genesis of Manic-Depressive States," *Contributions to Psycho-analysis*, p. 282, Melanie Klein.

"Mourning and its Relationship to Manic-Depressive States," *Contributions to Psycho-analysis*, p. 311, Melanie Klein. *Int.J.Psycho-Anal.*, vol. 21 (1940).

"A Contribution to the Theory of Anxiety and Guilt," *Developments in Psycho-analysis* (Chapter 8), Melanie Klein and others. *Int.J. Psycho-Anal.*, vol. 29 (1948).

"Some Theoretical Conclusions regarding the Emotional Life of the Infant," *Developments in Psycho-analysis* (Chapter 6), Melanie Klein and others.

HANNA SEGAL: "Notes on Symbol Formation," *Int.J.Psycho-Anal.*, vol. 38 (1957).

"A Psychoanalytic Contribution to Aesthetics," *Int.J.Psycho-Anal.* (1952), *New Directions in Psychoanalysis* (Chapter 16).

CHAPTER SEVEN

MANIC DEFENCES

THE EXPERIENCES of recurring depression and even despair which the infant is faced with when he feels that he has utterly and irretrievably ruined his mother and her breast, are intolerable, and the ego uses all the defences at its disposal against this state. These defences* fall under two headings—reparation and the manic defences. When depressive anxieties can be dealt with by the mobilization of reparative wishes, they lead to further growth of the ego.

This is not to say that the appearance of manic defences is in itself a pathological phenomenon; they have an important and positive part to play in development. The resolution of depression by reparation is a slow process and it takes a long time for the ego to acquire sufficient strength to feel confidence in its reparative capacities. Often the pain can only be overcome by manic defences which protect the ego from utter despair; when the pain and threat lessen, manic defences can gradually give way to reparation. When, however, manic defences are excessively strong, vicious circles are set in motion and points of fixation are formed which interfere with future development.

The organization of manic defences in the depressive position includes mechanisms which were already in evidence in the paranoid–schizoid position: splitting, idealization, projective identification, denial, etc. What distinguishes the later use of those defences is that they are highly organized in keeping with the more integrated state of the

* Whether reparation is to be considered a mechanism of defence will be discussed in the next chapter.

ego, and that they are specifically directed against the experience of depressive anxiety and guilt. This experience, is dependent on the fact that the ego has achieved a new relation to reality. The infant discovers his dependence on his mother, his sense of valuing her and, together with this dependence, he discovers his ambivalence and experiences intense feelings of fear of loss, mourning, pining and guilt in his relation to his object, external and internal.

It is against this whole experience that the manic defence organization is directed. Since the depressive position is linked with the experience of dependence on the object, manic defences will be directed against any feelings of dependence, which will be obviated, denied or reversed. Since depressive anxieties are linked with ambivalence, the infant will defend himself against ambivalence by a renewal of splitting of the object and the ego. Since depressive experience is linked with an awareness of an internal world, containing a highly valued internal object that can be damaged by one's own impulses, manic defences will be used in defence against any experience of having an internal world or of containing in it any valued objects, and against any aspect of the relation between the self and the object which threatens to contain dependence, ambivalence and guilt.

Technically, the manic defences are of overwhelming importance, since they are primarily directed against the experience of psychic reality, that is, against the whole aim of the analytical process, in so far as this aim is to bring insight and the full experience of psychic reality. Denial of psychic reality can be maintained by the re-awakening and strengthening of omnipotence and particularly of omnipotent control of the object.

The manic relation to objects is characterized by a triad of feelings—control, triumph and contempt. These feelings are directly related to, and defensive against depressive feelings of valuing the object and depending on it, and fear of loss and guilt. Control is a way of denying dependence, of not acknowledging it and yet of compelling the object to fulfil a need for dependence, since an object that is wholly controlled is, up a point, one that can be depended on. Triumph is a denial of depressive feelings of valuing and caring; it is linked with omnipotence and has two important aspects. One is connected with the primary attack made on the object in the depressive position, and with the triumph experienced in defeating this object, particularly if the attack is strongly determined by envy. Secondarily, the feeling of triumph is increased as part of the manic defences, because it keeps at bay those depressive feelings which would otherwise be aroused, such as pining and longing for and missing the object. Contempt for the object is again a direct denial of valuing the object, which is so important in the depressive position, and it acts as a defence against the experience of loss and of guilt. An object of contempt is not an object worthy of guilt, and the contempt that is experienced in relation to such an object becomes a justification for further attacks on it.

I should like to illustrate the operation of manic defences against the experience of dependence and threatened loss by some material presented by a patient preceding an analytical holiday. He was anxious lest I should terminate his treatment prematurely and the holiday be a prelude to the ending. In his associations, he referred frequently to his unsatisfactory feeding history and to the fact that his mother breast-fed him only for a day or two. He defended himself against his anxiety by manic defences. A middle-aged business man, he was usually successful in his business, but at that time he pulled off several particularly successful deals. He had phantasies of retiring to live abroad, where I would visit him during the holidays and would be lavishly entertained. Soon after mentioning this phantasy, he reported the following dream:

He was going to a pub and on the way he met Miss X, with whom he had had a passing affair many years ago. Miss X looked very down-trodden and unsuccessful and was obviously keen to renew her affair with him. He was embarrassed, a bit guilty and a little tempted, and he had a kind of compulsive sexual feeling that he often experienced towards women whom he found very unhappy or very unattractive.

His association first took him back to his youth. He was then under-manager in a chain store, very sure of himself and happy in managing people, particularly girls, and enjoying a feeling of power; he was very promiscuous and used to feel that shop-girls were the natural victims of young executives. Miss X worked in the dairy department. He used to find the dairy girls specially attractive. They wore a smart uniform in which they looked very pure and forbidding, and it gave him a particular feeling of triumph to get them to bed. He remembered all this with a great deal of unease and anxiety, as his sexual behaviour had completely altered during the analysis, and he was critical about his promiscuous past. Miss X made him particularly guilty, since he treated her in a worse way than most. He only slept with her once or twice and discarded her.

I interpreted that the girls working in the dairy represented the breast-feeding mother, who fed him only once or twice, and his relationship with Miss X as his retaliation in relation to his mother. As the pub in the dream was the pub on the corner of the street where I lived, I interpreted that Miss X was also myself in the transference, and connected the dream with the patient's phantasy of meeting me and entertaining me abroad. Behind the wish to entertain me was the wish both to reverse the situation of dependence— my becoming poor and ill-favoured and wanting to renew the acquaintance with him—and to have revenge. The patient suddenly laughed and said he realized why Miss X was associated in his mind with Miss Y, another girl with whom he had had a similarly short affair at another period of his life. Unlike his other girl friends, who were usually tall and attractive, these two were extremely short and both had enormous breasts, a combination which made them look almost ridiculous. He thought that maybe they were nothing more to him than a vagina connected with breasts.

He then thought that their being so small must mean that they represented a little girl cousin, several years younger than himself, with whom he had sexual games in childhood.

I interpreted that, in his phantasy, he attributed his mother's breast to the little girl, so as to protect himself against an experience of dependence, with the threat of loss that it implied. If he attributed the breasts to the little girl, he could possess them, control them, punish them, triumph over them and be able to use them without ever having to experience his dependence on them.

One can see in this material how the patient's manic defences protect him against depression. He is faced with the prospect of separation, in which he could experience the extent of his dependence, ambivalence and loss. He deals with it by phantasying that, in the person of his little girl cousin, the proto-type of all his later sexual objects, he possesses the breast. Love, dependence and guilt are completely denied, and are dealt with by devaluation and splitting. The little girl cousin is split into many unimportant girl friends, to be possessed and discarded at will.

Triumph as the main feature of a system of manic defences is shown in the following material presented by another patient who was also a typical manic personality.

Early on in his analysis he reported two dreams. In the first one he was somewhere in a desert watching people armed with butcher's knives cutting and eating flesh. Though he could not see exactly what they were eating, he saw that there were many corpses strewn around and he suspected that they were in fact eating human flesh. In a second dream, the same night, he was sitting at his boss's desk at the office. He felt unlike himself—he was big and fat and heavy, as though he had had a big meal.

The patient made a link between the two dreams and realized that he himself must have been the eater of the human flesh. He must have eaten his boss, standing for his father, and that is how he came to be sitting in the boss's chair and feeling so uncommonly big and heavy. These dreams illustrate what Freud meant by the "manic feast." The object is devoured and identified with and no loss or guilt for it is experienced. In the first dream the guilt is clearly dealt with by projection.

A few days later the patient reported a dream which

illustrates both the manic defences and the underlying depressive situation. It is important for the understanding of this dream to know that this patient had an unhappy early childhood. At the age of eighteen months, his mother brought him to London from the Continent, leaving his father behind. There was ample material in his analysis to show that he experienced this separation as his father's death. As soon as they arrived in London, his mother went into hospital, so that he was faced in quick succession with the loss of his father and of his mother.

Before reporting the dream, he began to laugh and had the greatest difficulty in controlling his laughter sufficiently to tell his dream. He said that he had had such a terribly funny dream during the night that he laughed in his dream and laughed on waking up and laughed now when he thought of it. The dream was as follows: he was in a barber's shop. There was a man called Joe sitting in the barber's chair shaved by a monkey. The monkey was very dark and wore spectacles—it was extremely funny! He felt quite friendly towards it: "It was such a sweet little monkey." But he said to the monkey that at home he had a little kitten who could shave very much better. He was afraid that the monkey's feelings were hurt, and he was sorry about it, because the monkey was likeable and he did not mean to be unpleasant. In a later part of the dream, he went into the barber's waiting-room and saw a long queue, with two men in it who were grumbling loudly and saying that the barbers in this country were not nearly as good as those on the Continent. They said that there were no queues in Europe, and they worked quicker there.

The patient's first associations were concerned with the two grumbling men. One was a comedy writer who wrote terribly funny farces; at this point, the patient interrupted himself to laugh again, remembering these very funny farces. This writer suffered from very severe periodic depressions, but this did not matter much because whenever he got them he had some E.C.T. and then he was as "right as rain." The other man who was grumbling was a surgeon, a gynae-cologist against whom the patient had been warned by a friend, who described him as "a real butcher." The patient himself made a link between this association and the previous dream in which there were people with butcher's knives.

Father Joe was a family friend who looked after him for a while when the family arrived from the Continent during his mother's illness. Father Joe was dead and the patient said that he had always felt vaguely guilty because, though he thought that this man had looked after him well and kindly, he had never kept contact with him or visited him when he had grown up and Father Joe was old and ill.

He connected the monkey with me and the kitten with his girl friend, called Kitty, who often competed with me and gave the patient her own interpretations. When he associated me with the monkey, he obviously felt uneasy and assured me in a very patronizing way that it was not an attack on me, his representing me by this monkey, since it was really such a likeable little monkey.

The queue at the barber's shop and the grumbling associated in his mind with the comparisons he often made between the swift and easy analysis that he thought was practised on the Continent compared with the enormous waiting lists and the long job of analysis here. He suddenly interrupted himself: last night he went for a walk in the East End and heard sirens in the distance and, whenever he heard sirens, he was terribly sad and moved—he didn't know why.

I have presented the main associations to the dream without any attempt to show the interplay between the patient's associations and the analyst's comments. The material is being given to show the main anxieties expressed and the defence mechanisms used. The underlying situation was that Father Joe was dead and the whole joke, the whole funniness of the dream, turned on this situation. The barber's shop represented an internal situation in which the patient felt that he contained a dead father whom he had neglected and abandoned. Analysis was the process whereby I, as the external father, tried to bring the dead internal father and the patient's internal world back to life. This analysis was ridiculed in the dream—it was a ridiculous joke to try and bring a dead man to life by shaving him. The analyst was represented as a ridiculous little monkey, who tried to revive a dead man by shaving him and even in that futile occupation was inferior to the kitten. The whole situation of depression and guilt in relation to the internal dead object was completely denied; as was the patient's dependence on the external father-analyst. This dependence was in fact enormous, since it was on his analyst that the patient depended to save him from his desperate internal situation. This situation of dependence was denied and reversed through the monkey being made little, ridiculous and jealous of the kitten.

The first part of the dream shows the denial of love, mourning and guilt in relation to the internal figure and of dependence in relation to the external one. In the next part of the dream concerned with the queue, further defences are represented, especially splitting and projective identification. The two grumbling men represent split-off and projected parts of the patient's own personality. The butchering surgeon stands for the patient's murderousness in relation to his father, which had become clear in the previous dreams; also, being a gynaecologist, he brings in the patient's anxieties about his mother, which came into focus in later sessions. The second man, associated with the comic writer, represents the patient's deep depression, as well as his manic denials. In fact, the patient thought his dream as funny as the writer's farces. Both parts of his personality, the hating one and the depressed one, are projected and split off from one another; even in the projected form, the patient cannot allow a link between the hatred and murder of the father, and the resulting depression. Also the depression of the writer is denied— he is "as right as rain." However, in the last part of the dream, the denial weakens, since the men are grumbling about having to wait: behind the denigration, the attacks and the criticism there is a partial admission of the patient's dependence, his anger at being kept waiting for his analysis between sessions, and lasting resentment at having been kept waiting for a vacancy. It was while the patient was giving his associations with this part of the dream that he suddenly

remembered hearing the sirens. When the depressive content of the dream and the manic defences were interpreted
to him his mood changed completely—he remembered the
sound of the sirens and associated them with the sirens he
must have heard during his first voyage and to the separation
from his father, which was experienced by him as a death.
It was then that he noticed the references in the dream to
the Continent.

At the end of the session, he suddenly remembered that
he had not reported that the previous night—that is, the
night of the dream—his father had suddenly become ill
and had been taken to hospital for an operation which the
patient feared he might not survive. It became abundantly
clear that the joke of the dream was a joke about the death
of his father, the whole dream being a manic way of dealing
with the underlying depression and anxiety.

This dream illustrates some of the dangers involved in
manic defences. The integration that the patient had obviously achieved in the depressive position had been disrupted by the splitting of his object and his ego. Projective
mechanisms had impoverished him. The whole-object
relation was threatened, the "monkey" figure was inhuman
—a partial regression to part-object relation. To maintain
the denial of his depressive anxiety and guilt, he had also
to deny his concern for the object, and this led to a renewal
of the attack on the object, his father being triumphed over
and attacked again with contempt and ridicule.

The foregoing material shows how the constant need to
renew the attack on the original object of love and dependence
sets in motion the vicious circle so characteristic of manic
defences. The object is originally attacked in an ambivalent
way in the depressive position. When guilt and loss in this
situation cannot be borne, the manic defences come into
play. The object is then treated with contempt, controlled
and triumphed over. Reparative activities cannot be carried out, and the ever-renewed attacks increase both the
destruction of the object and its vengeful retaliation, thereby
deepening depressive anxieties and making the underlying
depressive situation increasingly hopeless and persecutory.

Sometimes some concern for the object can be partially preserved and manic mechanisms can also be used in a reparative way, manic reparation presenting a very special problem of its own.

BIBLIOGRAPHY

JOAN RIVIERE: "A Contribution to the Analysis of the Negative Therapeutic Reaction," *Int.J.Psycho-Anal.*, vol. 17 (1936).
    "Magical Regeneration by Dancing," *Int.J.Psycho-Anal.*, vol. 11 (1930).
H. ROSENFELD: "On Drug Addiction," *Int.J.Psycho-Anal.*, vol. 41 (1960).

CHAPTER EIGHT

REPARATION

WHEN THE INFANT enters the depressive position and he is faced with the feeling that he has omnipotently destroyed his mother, his guilt and despair at having lost her awaken in him the wish to restore and recreate her in order to regain her externally and internally. The same reparative wishes arise in relation to other loved objects, external and internal. The reparative drives bring about a further step in integration. Love is brought more sharply into conflict with hate, and it is active both in controlling destructiveness and in repairing and restoring damage done. It is the wish and the capacity for the restoration of the good object, internal and external, that is the basis of the ego's capacity to maintain love and relationships through conflicts and difficulties. It is also the basis for creative activities, which are rooted in the infant's wish to restore and recreate his lost happiness, his lost internal objects and the harmony of his internal world.

Reparative phantasies and activities resolve the anxieties of the depressive position. The acute intensity of depressive anxiety is mitigated by repeated experiences of loss and recovery of the object. The re-appearance of the mother after absences, which are felt as death, and the continued love and care the infant receives from his environment, make him more aware of the resilience of his external objects and less frightened of the omnipotent effects of the attacks he makes on them in his phantasies. His own growth and the restorations that he carries out in relation to his objects bring an increased trust in his own love, his own capacity to restore his internal object and to retain it as good, even in the face of deprivation by external objects. This in turn makes him more capable of experiencing deprivation without being overwhelmed by hatred. His own hatred also becomes less frightening as his belief increases that his love can restore what his hatred has destroyed. Through the repetition of experiences of loss and recovery, felt partly as destruction by hatred, and recreation through love, the good object becomes gradually better assimilated into the ego, because, in so far as the ego has restored and recreated the object internally, it is increasingly owned by the ego and can be assimilated by it and contribute to its growth. Hence the enrichment of the ego through the process of mourning. Together with these emotional changes, growing skill and capacity in real external activities bring repeated assurance about the ego's reparative capacities. Reality testing is increased when reparative drives are in the ascendant: the infant watches with concern and anxiety the effect of his phantasies on external objects; and an important part of his reparation is learning to give up omnipotent control of his object and accept it as it really is.

I shall illustrate by a dream some aspects of reparation, particularly in relation to internal objects. The patient was a manic-depressive and she had the dream at a time when, feeling very much improved after several years' analysis, she was considering terminating it.

She dreamt that she was driving in her car to work. There was some anxiety at this point in the dream because the electric current was cut off, but she realized that she had a torch battery of her own and that the battery was in working order. When she arrived at work, she waited for a doctor to turn up to help her; but when he turned up he had a broken arm in a sling and was useless. She slowly realized that the work she was supposed to carry out was the opening up of an enormous mass grave. She started digging alone by the light of her little torch. Gradually, as she dug, she realized that not all the people buried in this grave were dead. Moreover, to her great encouragement, those who were still alive immediately began to dig with her. At the end of the dream, she had a very strong feeling that two things had been achieved; one was that anyone who was still alive had been rescued from this mass grave, and had become her helper; and, secondly, that those people who were dead could now be taken out of the anonymous grave and (this seemed extremely important to her in the dream) could now be buried properly with their names on the grave.

At some point in the dream, she thought that all the victims in the grave were women.

One of her associations with the mass grave was having read a book about the Warsaw ghetto. It is impossible here to go into all her associations, and this one had a very long history. Her mother was partially Jewish, and her unconscious anti-Semitism had come a great deal into the analysis. Mass graves or masses of corpses had appeared often before, usually associated with a murderous attack on her mother and myself in an oedipal situation. The doctor with the broken arm had many associations in relation to her current life, but he mainly represented her father, castrated by her in an early oedipal situation and unable to help her to restore her mother. The cutting off of the electric current represented the stopping of the treatment, and her own torch battery she associated with her own insight, which she had acquired through the analysis.

Briefly, this dream represented to her the gradual solving of her depressive anxieties. Going to work with her little torch meant facing by herself the full extent of her depressive situation, facing her vicious attacks on her mother and all the mother representatives, which led to the mass grave inside her, the anonymous depression, when she did not know what she was mourning for. The work of mourning in this dream consisted of rescuing and restoring what could be rescued and restored. The objects which she had restored immediately turned into helpers; that is, the objects first destroyed by her and then restored became assimilated by her and strengthened her own ego.

But not everything that had been destroyed could be restored. She also had to face those situations in which the object was really dead, like many of her relatives, and situations in which she felt that she had done harm which could not be undone. And here the important point is that each of those situations and persons had to be properly named and buried, that is, they had to be recognized and mourned without denial, not lost in a mass grave. When properly buried, they could eventually be given up and did not have to be kept magically alive, so that the patient's libido might be free of her fixation on them.

There is, however, an ominous element in the dream indicating a still active manic organization. This element is the patient's insistence that she has to do it "all by herself." This is not only a recognition of her need to become independent of analysis, it is also an insistence on her own omnipotence. The father figure in the dream remains castrated and is not allowed to help. The mother is to be restored by the patient all by herself, without any help from father, a clear indication of difficulties ahead in relation to the oedipal situation, which necessitates the restoration of the parental couple.

I have mentioned, in the previous chapter, that reparation itself may be part of the manic defences. In such a case, an attempt is made to repair the object in a manic and omnipotent way. It can then be partly treated as an object of concern. Non-manic and manic reparation differ, however, in important respects. Reparation proper can hardly be considered a defence, since it is based on the recognition of psychic reality, the experiencing of the pain that this reality causes and the taking of appropriate action to relieve it in phantasy and reality. It is, in fact, the very reverse of a defence, it is a mechanism important both for the growth of the ego and its adaptation to reality.

Manic reparation is a defence in that its aim is to repair the object in such a way that guilt and loss are never experienced. An essential feature of manic reparation is that it has to be done without acknowledgement of guilt, and therefore under special conditions. For instance, manic reparation is never done in relation to primary objects or internal objects, but always in relation to more remote objects; secondly, the object in relation to which reparation is done must never be experienced as having been damaged by oneself; thirdly, the object must be felt as inferior, dependent and, at depth, contemptible. There can be no true love or esteem for the object or objects that are being repaired, as this would threaten the return of true depressive feelings. Manic reparation can never be completed, because, if it were complete, the object fully restored would again become lovable and esteemed, and free from the manic person's omnipotent control and contempt. Fully restored to independence and again endowed with value, it would be exposed once more to immediate attack with hatred and contempt.

Because of these conditions, the underlying guilt which manic reparation seeks to alleviate is, in fact, not relieved, and the reparation brings no lasting satisfaction. The objects that are being repaired are unconsciously, and sometimes consciously, treated with hatred and contempt and are invariably felt as ungrateful and, at least unconsciously, are dreaded as potential persecutors.

One can sometimes see this kind of manic reparation in charitable institutions, when, for instance, those in control see themselves as spending charity and reparation on unworthy and ungrateful people whom they feel to be essentially bad and dangerous.

I should like to show the gradual change-over from manic to true reparation in the material of a four-year-old patient. The sessions I wish to describe happened a few days before the summer holiday, when Ann was particularly concerned with her attacks on me and the need for reparation. My going away on holiday represented for her the parental intercourse and mother's pregnancy. In her play the box of paints came to represent primarily her mother's breast, and the drawer in which I kept her toys her mother's body full of babies. In the days preceding the two sessions I am going to describe, she furiously attacked the box of paints, digging out the paints with her knife, mixing them up and dissolving them in water. She would then use the dirty coloured water to "drown" the little toys in the drawer. This was interpreted to her mainly as representing an attack on her mother's breast with teeth and nails, making holes in it, messing it up and using the messed-up milk turned into urine and faeces to attack her mother's body, and mess and drown the new babies. The reason for the attack was the deprivation of the holiday and her jealousy and envy when she imagined that I, standing for her mother, would go away to have sexual intercourse and more babies.

An important aspect of this aggressive situation was Ann's attack on words. She would either drown my words in shrieking and singing, or shout and repeat them meaninglessly, breaking up into syllables or chanting "blah, blah, blah." I interpreted this attack on my words as being equivalent to a biting attack on mother's breast and sometimes on the parental intercourse, and her shrieking and shouting "Blah, Blah," as the production of bad faeces—which she was throwing at me.

Towards the end of one of the sessions, she asked me to draw a little girl. The little girl, she said, was Ann and she was going to paint her bottom. Thereupon she put an enormous mass of brown paint all over and between the little girl's legs. When this was interpreted as the stools she was making out of food, she quickly made a similar brown mass coming out of the little girl's head. Whereupon I could interpret to her that, when she was hating me, she was doing in her head with my words what she felt she was doing in her tummy to Mummy's food. She confirmed that by saying that blah, blah was really plop, plop (her baby word for stools).

In the next session, manic reparation was predominant. She came into the room, went immediately to her box of paints and realized that by now it was unusable. She asked me if I had got a new box for her, and, when she saw that I had not, took it to the draining board and said "You must mend it very quickly and make it just exactly as it was before." She brought some white glue powder, put some of the glue in the squares that used to contain paint, realized that it would not do and said "You must do it for me, but very quickly, I'll do the singing." As I filled the squares with white powder and a little water, and spread the remainder of the paint to give some colour to the powder, she was jumping from foot to foot, singing very loudly "Easy, weasy, let's get busy," getting more and more excited and shouting to me to hurry. She immediately accepted the interpretation that I was to do it by magic and said that her song was a spell and magic was very quick.

The emphasis was on reparation done by magic, quickly, and on getting the box "exactly as before." The reason for this was so that guilt and loss could be denied; reparation must be so swift and complete that Ann would have no time to mourn or to feel guilty. The reparation that I could do on the box was obviously not nearly magical enough to satisfy these needs. Several times she interrupted her singing and pretended to go to sleep, hoping not to see the destruction of the paint box, while the relatively slow reparation was in progress. She wanted to wake up to find it all magically restored, but her anxiety and impatience would not let her go to sleep properly and after a minute or two she would rush again to the draining board and take a peep at the paint box.

Behind the excitement, anger was rising. Over and over again she would take the box out of my hand, thinking she could do it more quickly herself, then get furious with the box, wash out all the work that had already been done, give the box back to me and then get furious with me for not doing it quickly enough. All the time she was controlling me and shouting at me more and more angrily.

Her anger with the box was her anger with the original attacked object—with mother's breast, which, by not letting itself be repaired quickly enough, was exposing her to the painful feeling of loss and guilt and therefore arousing a further onslaught of hatred. Her relation to me was complicated. To begin with, she wished to deny all dependence on me and hoped to repair the box by her own magic. She was driven, however, to seek my help. She could use my help only by treating me as a part-object, wholly controlled by herself. My impression was that I, as a part-object, was the penis with whose help Ann wanted magically to restore her mother. But this object that she needed and used for her reparation had to be controlled completely, and she hated it more and more since she could not control and use it in the way she wanted to. Furthermore, both the box and I were felt as being increasingly persecutory; since she endowed me with magic powers, she felt that my not repairing the box in the way she wanted might have been done on purpose to spite her, in retaliation for her ruthless attempts to control me.

Right through this session, her attack on my words was becoming more and more frantic. This was easily understandable, for my speaking and interpreting were felt by Ann as an assertion of my independent existence as a whole person, with thoughts and ideas of my own, and on whose help Ann herself depended, whereas Ann wanted me to be only a part-object completely under control. Furthermore, my interpretation, linking Ann's reparative activities with her previous damaging of the box, confronted her with the very truth that she sought to avoid, that is, that the need for repair was the result of her previous aggression. Since her reparation was wholly oriented so as to deny this fact, my interpretations were not felt as a help, but as a constant interference in her magic reparative activities. As the hour went on, however, she became a little calmer and was eventually able to listen to a complete interpretation, in which I tried to relate her present activities and feelings to the previous session and to the coming holiday.

The next session shows a complete change of mood, in which manic mechanisms recede and true reparation sets in. As soon as she came into the room, she went again to the box, opened it, gave a little sigh and said "Isn't it a pity it's so spoilt?," then turned to me and said "Let's try to mend it together." This time she did not insist either on the speed or on the completeness of the process, nor did she want the box to be exactly as before. With the white powder and water and a little paint that was still left over, she and I managed to restore sufficient coloured matter to use the box of paints for another day. Then she moved to the table, asked for paper and began painting a house. Since she could not as yet paint a complete house by herself, she asked me to help. She also asked me for crayons to make up for the inadequacy of the paints. In that way she partly drew and partly painted a house. She said it was a beautiful house and asked me to draw the outline of another bigger house around it. I asked her if she thought the little house inside the big house was herself inside Mummy, but Ann showed me the pointed roof of the little house and said with great conviction that the house was Daddy inside Mummy. I could then interpret to her that repairing the box of paints meant repairing Mummy's body and that she felt she needed Daddy's, that is, my help in order to make Mummy all right again. The Daddy house inside the Mummy house represented Mummy and Daddy being restored, and re-stored to one another, Daddy making Mummy better and giving her new babies. She then turned the sheet of paper over and showed me that the back was covered with a brown mess of paint that she had previously spilled on the table and she said "It's all a mess again." I interpreted that as soon as she allowed Daddy to make Mummy better by being with her and inside her she felt jealous again and wanted to mess them up with her stools. She asked for more crayons and wanted to draw more houses. As we drew and painted the houses, she several times dropped cut bits of paper and wood shavings on to my dress, each time cleaning me up carefully. Whenever she did it, she would half laughingly say "Oh dear, I have done it again, we've got to do the cleaning again and again." In that way, she gave me an opportunity to interpret directly in the transference her repeated attacks on me, and the task of reparation she was faced with if she wanted me to continue being a good analyst to her. After a time, she painted a pattern and asked me to help her name the colours which she was trying to memorize. I could then interpret to her that I was the father whom Ann needed to restore her internal mother and bring order into her internal world; and related her request to name the colours to her acknowledgement that the real help I was able to give her was in naming the different feelings inside her helping her to know them, to differentiate them and, therefore, to feel more able to control them.

One can see this session as being in complete contrast
to the previous one; in this session, too, Ann was concerned
with the reparation of the box, representing her mother,
using the help of the analyst, representing her father. But
whereas in the previous session the reparation was magical,
based on a complete denial of guilt and concern, with a
ruthless attitude to the mother as an object of reparation
and the father treated as a part object, in this session her
reparation resulted from an experience of guilt and loss.
She began by saying that it was a pity the box was spoilt.
With this change went also a changed attitude to myself;
she accepted me as a whole person, father, who made
reparation to herself and to her mother, and helped her to
do such reparation as she could. There was an acknowledgement of need and dependence on both parents, and of the
necessity to have them both restored and to have their help
in the process of reparation. At the same time, there was
an acknowledgement not only of aggression in the past,
but of continuing aggression. When the parents were allowed
to come together as the two houses, aggression broke out
again. With the acknowledgement of the psychic reality
of jealous and aggressive feeling went the recognition that
reparation is a difficult task. In her play of throwing wood
shavings on me and then cleaning me up, she admitted that
the battle with her aggression had to go on all the time and
could not be won magically once and for all. At the same
time, she realized that the recognition of psychic reality
is a help. There was full insight here that the analyst's help
did not consist in giving her new paints, paper, etc., but in
"naming," that is, in enabling her to sort out her feelings
and impulses and her relationships with external and internal
figures. The step that Ann took between these two sessions
was a crucial one, in that it enabled her to give up at least
for the time being a magical use of her analysis for a more
realistic and insightful one.

It is interesting to note that both the dream of the adult
patient and the material of the little girl bring in the
"naming" as an important element in reparation. The
"naming" in both cases represents the acceptance of reality,

the fundamental element of real reparation, which is lacking in manic reparation. The acceptance of psychic reality involves the renunciation of omnipotence and magic, the lessening of splitting and the withdrawal of projective identification. It means the acceptance of the idea of separateness—the differentiation of one's own self from one's parents, with all the conflicts that it implies. It also involves, as part of reparation, allowing one's objects to be free, to love and restore one another without depending on oneself. All or most of these elements are lacking when the reparation is a part of manic defences against depressive anxieties.

BIBLIOGRAPHY

Melanie Klein: "Infantile Anxiety Situations reflected in a Work of Art and in the Creative Impulse," *Contributions to Psycho-analysis*, p. 223, Melanie Klein, *Int.J.Psycho-Anal.*, vol. 10 (1931).

"Contributions to the Psycho-genesis of Manic-Depressive States," *Contributions to Psycho-analysis*, p. 282, Melanie Klein.

"Mourning and its Relationship to Manic-Depressive States," *Contributions to Psycho-analysis*, p. 311, Melanie Klein. *Int.J.Psycho-Anal.*, vol. 21 (1940).

"A Contribution to the Theory of Anxiety and Guilt," *Developments in Psycho-analysis* (Chapter 8), Melanie Klein and others. *Int.J. Psycho-Anal.*, vol. 29 (1948).

"Some Theoretical Conclusions regarding the Emotional Life of the Infant," *Developments in Psycho-analysis* (Chapter 6), Melanie Klein and others.

Hanna Segal: "A Psycho-analytic Approach to Aesthetics," *New Directions in Psycho-analysis* (Chapter 16), Melanie Klein and others. *Int.J.Psycho-Anal.*, vol. 33 (1952).

"Notes on Symbol Formation," *Int.J.Psycho-Anal.*, vol. 38 (1957).

Joan Riviere: "A Contribution to the Analysis of the Negative Therapeutic Reaction," *Int.J.Psycho-Anal.*, vol. 17 (1936).

"Magical Regeneration by Dancing," *Int.J.Psycho-Anal.*, vol. 11 (1930).

H. Rosenfeld: "On Drug Addiction," *Int.J.Psycho-Anal.*, vol. 41 (1960).

CHAPTER NINE

THE EARLY STAGES OF THE OEDIPUS COMPLEX

IT IS IMPLICIT in Melanie Klein's definition of the depressive position, that the oedipus complex begins to develop during this phase, of which it is an integral part. When the mother is perceived as a whole object, there is a change not only in the infant's relation to his mother, but also in his perception of the world. People are recognized by him as individual and separate and as having relationships with one another; in particular, the infant becomes aware of the important link that exists between his father and his mother. This sets the stage for the oedipus complex. But the infant's perception of other people's relationships is very different from the perception of an adult or even an older child. As projections colour all his perceptions, when he senses the libidinal link between his parents he projects in to them his own libidinal and aggressive desires. When he is under the sway of his own powerful impulses he phantasies his parents in almost uninterrupted intercourse and the nature of this intercourse will vary with the fluctuations of his own impulses. He will phantasy his parents as exchanging gratifications, oral, urethral, anal or genital, according to the prevalence of his own impulses which he projects into them. This situation, in which the infant perceives his parents in terms of his own projections, gives rise to feelings of the most acute deprivation, jealousy and envy, since the parents are perceived as constantly giving one another precisely those gratifications which the infant wishes for himself.

The child reacts to the situation by an increase of his

aggressive feelings and phantasies. The parents in his phantasies will be attacked by all the aggressive means at his disposal, and they will be perceived in phantasy as being destroyed. Since introjection is very active during this stage of development, those attacked and destroyed parents are immediately introjected and felt by the child as part of his internal world. That is, in the depressive situation the infant has not only to deal with a destroyed internal breast and mother, but also with the internal destroyed parental couple of the early oedipal situation.

The following dreams illustrate the early oedipal situation in a very depressed patient. The symptoms she complained of most at that time were a feeling of deadness inside, an inability to take things in, particularly her analysis, and a general feeling of paralysis and lifelessness. One day she reported three dreams dreamt consecutively.

First dream: she dreamt that she was eating cherry jam and she had a horrible feeling in her mouth of the bits of cherry and cherry juice dribbling out of it. She felt as though she had bitten off bleeding bits of something. She thought that it was all the fault of Dr. X.

He association was that she had had supper the night before with Miss P and that Miss P told her that a Dr. Y had asked her to give a series of lectures on psychology in his hospital. The patient was not aware of any jealousy. Dr. X is a young man with whom the patient had been in love before she was depressed and of whose wife she was intensely jealous. Miss P is a very good figure in the patient's life and usually represents the good aspect of the analyst and the mother. Even when the patient is very depressed she can bear to see Miss P though she feels that she cannot establish any real contact or "take anything from her." The night preceding the dream she had no appetite though the supper Miss P provided was very good. Her second association with the dream connected Dr. Y with Dr. X, and Miss P's giving lectures to myself giving lectures at the Institute. But the strongest feeling of the dream was about the bleeding bitten-up bits. These, she felt, were what she had changed Miss P's supper into. As her associations proceeded, it became clear that Miss P stood for me and the mother and her supper stood for the breast, and that as soon as Dr. Y was mentioned, stirring in the patient a powerful unconscious oedipal jealousy, she felt that she had attacked the breast with her teeth and turned it into the bleeding bits represented by the cherry jam.

Second dream: she was eating porridge from a nice little bowl which had little white birds on it, but as soon as she had started eating the porridge, she felt disgusted and frightened because she found three objects in the porridge which cut her lips and stuck in her throat. The three objects were a little broken-up cross, a torn purse and a cage with hooks.

The little birds on the bowl she associated with my name. As to the three objects, after some resistance she associated the cross with her own crossness, and the purse with the vagina. I had to supply the suggestion that the cage with the hooks represented the vagina containing the penis.

This dream continues to bring out the theme of her inability to "take in," as related to her difficulties at the breast when faced with the oedipal situation. The bowl of porridge again represents the breast, but this breast is for her full of the sexual parts of the parents as though the intercourse was taking place right inside the breast. The intercourse is felt as very bad and the bits of the parental genitals are felt to be not only damaged (the torn purse, the broken cross) but also vengeful and damaging. As in the first dream, she is faced with the situation in which oedipal anxieties seem to interfere with her taking in the good food from the mother and mother-figures.

These two dreams illustrate the interaction between the relationship to the breast and oedipal problems—the influx of oedipal envy and jealousy leads to an increase of attacks on the breast and, with it, to an inhibition in feeding and a deepening of depression. Conversely, there was other material which showed how her ambivalent relation to the breast increased her oedipal difficulties, in that the breast-mother had never been sufficiently established as a good internal object for the patient to identify with.

The third dream, dreamt the same night, deals with another aspect of her depression—her feelings of paralysis and deadness. In this dream, she was at a garden party and she saw a man going to a brothel "to do a 'jig jig.' " Then she was in something that was like a secret garden and she saw two birds beak to beak, but they were immobile because their beaks were transfixed by the beak of a third bird. The two birds were white, the third bird which was transfixing them she didn't remember clearly, but she thought it was black. Her associations were with Graham Green's *The End of the Affair*, in which a love affair ends in a suicide. It is in this book that the expression "to do a jig jig" occurs, in connection with a debased form of intercourse; the two birds were again associated with my name.

There was a lot of background to this dream. The patient used to have an evening hour, as she had to be taken on with some urgency and I had no day-time vacancy. In the previous week I had been able to change her evening appointment for a more usual daytime hour, and she told me how glad she was at the thought that now I would be able to spend my evenings in the garden with my husband. The secret garden in her dream is a reference to a book she read in childhood and which she had often referred to in her analysis. At more hopeful times she had a feeling that there was a secret garden inside her, in which things were good and alive, and if only she could penetrate there, she would be well again. The dream made her particularly depressed when she realized on waking that in her dream she found the secret garden, but the birds inside it were not alive, they were paralysed.

The dream represents her attack on myself and my husband, standing for the parents in the oedipal situation. My garden in which I was to spend evenings with my husband becomes the garden party of the dream. Our intercourse becomes a sordid affair, in which my husband goes to the brothel "to do the 'jig jig'," and commits suicide. The alternative to this situation is the secret garden; in it she incorporates the parents in intercourse—the two white birds beak to beak—and immobilizes them, paralyses their intercourse. The secret garden represents her internal world and particularly her genital, in which she contains the paralysed parental figures and in identification with them has to be frigid and immobile. In the external situation, she cannot turn either to her father, who has become a very bad sexual object, nor to her mother, whose breast is felt to be destroyed in the oedipal rivalry.

This dream has more overtly genital elements than the two previous ones, but it has all the characteristics of a very early oedipal complex, the parental couple being dealt with in a manner typical of the depressive position: she attacks them ambivalently, introjects them into the internal world and partly identifies with them. The paralysis of the parental couple and her idealization of them in this paralysed state is a manic defence.

Against the situation of deprivation, jealousy, envy, acute destructiveness and the resulting depression, the defences I described as pertaining to the paranoid–schizoid and depressive positions respectively are, of course, deployed. Denial, splitting and idealization may take various forms. There may be a splitting as between good, asexual parents and bad sexual ones. A splitting between mother and father may occur, one parent becoming ideal, while the other is felt as a persecutor. This last form of splitting may closely resemble a genital, oedipal situation, except for the extreme idealization of the desired parent and extreme hatred and persecution experienced in relation to the rival parent. Also, with such extremes of idealization and persecution, the rôle of the ideal object and the persecutor usually shifts rapidly from one parent to the other.

An important rôle is played in the early Oedipus complex by the phantasy of the combined parents. This phantasy appears first when the infant becomes aware of his mother as a whole object but does not fully differentiate the father from her; he phantasies the penis or the father as a part of his mother, his idealization of her makes him see her as the container of everything desirable, breast, babies, penises. Envious attacks and projections can make this figure into a threatening persecutor.

As the parents become more fully differentiated and their sexual intercourse arouses jealousy and envy the child may regress to this phantasy of the combined parents as a defence. The parental relationship is denied and in omnipotent phantasy changed into a combined parental figure. At the same time the child's aggression aroused by the intercourse is projected into this figure. The parents in hated intercourse become a hateful, threatening monster. It is this terrifying figure which often forms the core of children's nightmares and delusions of persecution.

It will be clear from what I have said so far that in Melanie Klein's view the child has an awareness of both the male and female genital from quite early on and that the phallic phase and the phantasy of the phallic woman are defensive structures—one of the versions of the combined parents.

A combined parent-figure appears in the dream dreamt by a patient in a manic phase, just prior to the summer holiday. She dreamt that she was at a fair and there was a little sideshow. At this sideshow there was a monstrously fat, pregnant man with enormous teeth, who was exhibiting himself and making speeches. Everybody around was laughing and she herself did not know whether to be sorry for the man, disgusted, or whether to laugh with everybody else. Very unusually, for this patient, she had no direct associations with the dream; much of the hour was taken up with secretly attacking me with contempt and ridicule, but there was no direct link with the ridiculous situation in the dream. Near the end of the hour she mentioned, however, that she had just heard something about me. A few weeks previously, someone had told her that I was going to give a lecture in Cambridge. She thought it would be in one of the big colleges, but she had just heard that it was merely going to be a talk to a student organization. This association immediately clarified the dream. The sideshow was the student's organization and the fat, pregnant man who was exhibiting himself was myself reading the paper. The student's society, to which she couldn't go, had become the miserable little sideshow. We knew, from previous material, that the patient was extremely envious of my reading any papers; it represented to her my masculine potency and my female fertility at one and the same time. At times the papers represented babies made jointly by me and my husband in good intercourse.

This situation of the parents having good intercourse and the mother producing the baby is for her the peak of a situation of jealousy and envy. She deals with it by combining the two parents into a monstrous figure. She also projects into this figure her own oral aggression, endowing it with enormous teeth. Such a figure was very often experienced by the patient as an enormously threatening and persecuting one. In this dream, however, she can deal with it by manic contempt and ridicule. The monstrous pregnant man as a figure of fun is a denial of her jealousy and envy of the parental situation, an attack on it with contempt and ridicule, and a denial of persecution in relation to this figure, which is both attacked and contains the projected aggression, by manic control and ridicule.

This is, of course, an extremely precarious situation, and further dreams showed that when contempt cannot be maintained and fear appears, the patient deals with it in her manic phase by identifying with this threatening figure; thus, a few nights later, she produced a dream in which she was clearly identified with a powerful lorry that was getting out of control.

In the dreams I have just described, coming from patients who were very ill, we can observe the very early stage of the oedipus complex. This early stage is characterized by the acuteness of the ambivalence, the predominance of oral trends and the uncertain choice of the sexual object. It would be difficult to conclude from either of those dreams which of the parents is the more desired and which is treated as a rival. Both are desirable and both are hated, and the predominant attack is on their mutual relationship. In the course of development the choice of parent will vary and both libidinal and aggressive aims will vary, both in the choice of object and in the importance of the libidinal zone. Libidinal aims develop from the early oral aim which is the oral incorporation of the breast or penis, through urethral and anal desires to full genital desire. We are now inclined to think that genital trends are present very much earlier on than used to be supposed, though they do not predominate till later in the infant's development. This development from the oral to the genital position does not happen in any direct or straightforward way; there is constant fluctuation. The child's own physiological development as well as the frustration of his early desires drive him on to more advanced ones. Frustration and anxiety encountered in the new position make him regress again. Thus there are constant fluctuations, overlapping and conflict between different desires until gradually genital supremacy is established and the child has to experience and work through the full impact of genital jealousy. Similarly, there is constant fluctuation in the choice of the predominantly desired parent and already in the oral situation the basis is laid both for heterosexual and for homosexual object-choice.

To both the boy and the girl infant the first object of desire is the mother's breast, and the father is perceived to begin with as a rival. But, in view of the persecutory and depressive anxieties experienced by the child in relation to the mother and her breast, the father's penis quickly becomes both to the little girl and the little boy an alternative object of oral desire to be turned to away from the breast.

For the little girl, this first oral turning to the penis is a heterosexual move paving the way to the genital situation and the wish to incorporate the penis in her vagina. But at the same time it contributes to her homosexual trends in that, at that stage of development, the oral desire is linked with incorporation and identification, and the wish to be fed by the penis is accompanied by a wish to possess a penis of her own.

For the little boy this turning to the penis of his father as an alternative to his mother's breast is primarily a move towards passive homosexuality, but at the same time this incorporation of his father's penis helps in his identification with him and in that way strengthens his heterosexuality.

It would be too complicated to go into all the possible

combinations of the oral relation to the parents and the various ways in which it develops into the genital one. It need only be said that very soon oral situations are accompanied by anal, urethral and genital desires, and that this turning to the father's penis, both for the little girl and for the little boy, soon develops into a genital situation, a wish for intercourse with him and the desire to receive babies from him.

At the same time, of course, genital feelings grow in relation to the mother. The longing to regain the early breast relationship gets transmuted into a desire for genital union; and depressive feelings in relation to the damage felt to be done to the mother's body and to her breast are a stimulus to the development of genital trends, and with them the wish to restore the mother's body by genital intercourse which would restore to her the penis, the babies and fill her breasts with milk. This relation to the mother may be felt predominantly as to an external object, in which case she becomes the aim of genital desires, heterosexual in the boy and homosexual in the girl; or these wishes may be mainly directed at the internal mother with whom the child identifies. In the latter case this wish to restore the mother by genitality increases heterosexual desires in the little girl and homosexual ones in the little boy.

As development proceeds the genital aim becomes predominant, and with its predominance the choice between the two parents will fluctuate less and less, and a more definite and more lasting choice will be made of the parent of the opposite sex as an object for libidinal desires, while both rivalry and identification increase in relation to the parent of the same sex. A growing reality sense brings with it the perception of the infant's own sex, and helps towards a partial renunciation of homosexual desires and an acceptance of whichever sex the child is. Thus the stage is gradually set for the classical oedipus complex in genital terms.

Masturbation, which has been pre-genital or genital, gradually becomes predominantly or exclusively genital; the masturbation phantasies which were to begin with connected with oral, anal and urethral phantasies even when masturbation was genital, become also more consistently concerned with genital sexual intercourse. The boy's phantasies centre on intercourse with his mother and castration fears; the girl's on intercourse with father and anxiety about attacks by her mother. These anxieties in turn bring regressive moves until genitality is more fully established.

But of course nothing in the development of the individual is ever fully overcome or ever fully lost, so that the genital oedipal situation will bear traces of earlier desires, including their symbolical representations, which will soon become apparent in analysis. The genital act will be seen to incorporate and symbolize all earlier forms of relationship. We also know that the heterosexual choice is never completely final and that, accompanying the classical positive oedipus complex, we shall always find in a repressed symbolized form its counterpart, the negative oedipus complex.

The following material illustrates some of the complexity behind an apparently positive genital oedipus complex.

Preceding the Christmas break, which in the patient's mind was connected with phantasies of the analyst's pregnancy, the patient reported the following dream.

"He was going to take a holiday in South Africa. The ticket cost £2, but he wasn't sure that he had the money. He looked again and found that he had a box of square foreign money and there was a feeling of something magic about it, the money was quite inexhaustible. He was sitting in a lounge waiting for the time to go to the plane and he bought himself two beers. He could also have whisky if he wanted to. He felt very rich and comfortable and walked slowly to the plane while somebody commented on his smart appearance. In front of the plane he saw his sister with her son."

His associations centred first on his meeting the previous night with a South African psycho-analyst, Dr. S, who had come to England to continue his studies. He felt very inferior to Dr. S, considering him to be a far more serious and valuable person than himself. Yet Dr. S was living in comparative poverty, working very hard, sometimes even going hungry and suffering from the cold climate. Compared

with him my patient felt very rich and comfortable and
particularly guilty since, in contrast to Dr. S, he felt his own
activities were mainly directed towards getting rich. He had
a number of associations with South Africa as a warm,
mysterious country with jungles, and to his own longing
for warmth. The money, he thought, represented his
potency and the key to those things he longed for. He also
wondered whether I would go for a holiday to South Africa
this Christmas, as I was taking a slightly longer holiday
than usual.

On the face of it the dream presented a straightforward
oedipal dream. Over the Christmas holiday the patient is
left out in the cold while his analyst is supposed to travel
to warm countries in company with Dr. S, standing for the
husband or the lover. In the dream and associations to it,
this situation is reversed. Dr. S is thrown out to suffer
cold and hunger while the patient travels to South Africa
with his analyst; and it is he who has the potent penis—the
money with which to achieve this end. The patient practi-
cally interpreted the dream himself and it produced very
little anxiety. All his anxiety was centred on one detail
of the dream—the square money. Money was always an
anxious topic for this patient; much of his omnipotence
and border-line dishonesty was centred on it.

His first association was that the square money was magic
since in the dream it felt quite inexhaustible; secondly, it
occurred to him that there was no such thing as square
money; "square" was also associated with square deals and
honesty; he felt that his money was magical and omnipotent and couldn't have been got in a "square" manner.
He also felt that he might be using it in a dishonest fashion.
His later association to "square" led him to childhood
memories. In the district where he lived some places were
called "square" though they were not so in shape. One that
was particularly important in his childhood was forbidden
territory, since the boys who lived there were hostile to
the boys in his own street. To get there you had to go through
a long, narrow passage, and he felt it was mysterious and
very dangerous. Going into it meant going into a fight.

Another point was that the boys who lived in the square were richer and better class than my patient and his friends.

All these associations were fraught with anxiety, and it soon transpired why. The cheat about his money was two-fold; first, the money, representing the penis, was acquired in a magic and wrong way by displacing and robbing his father; second, the cheat was in the use of his penis and the apparent aim of having intercourse—the real aim was to get back through the narrow passage into the womb and occupy the position of the new baby. Being in South Africa represented being in the womb and acquiring all the riches from the inside of his mother's body. He associated the two glasses of beer with the breasts, and the whisky that he could also have with the penis. So behind the apparent genital oedipal aim was the guilty wish to acquire the riches contained inside the woman.

This theme occupied the next few days. Then, the night before the day he would expect to get my bill, he dreamt another dream in which somebody sent him a cheque for £89 or £98. He first associated eight and nine with the months of pregnancy. He also thought of some cheques he had received, two of which were "post mortem," from the estates of people who had died. He felt very uneasy about these cheques. A large part of the session was concerned with his anxiety about the future, in which it became clear that his predominant feeling was that he would remain in analysis, which at that point represented his being the baby, until he could be richer, bigger, better than his analyst.

This dream, like the preceding one, is concerned with reversal; this time he reverses the situation of pregnancy. He is the pregnant mother; he receives the cheques, standing here for pregnancy, and the cheques are called "post-mortem," i.e. after the analyst's death, whose place as the pregnant mother he takes. His idea of being in analysis until he becomes richer and better than his analyst is connected with a phantasy that he will stay as the baby in the womb until he has taken in so much that his rich, pregnant mother will die and he will become her. So that his genital position (and one of his presenting symptoms was compulsive promiscuity) is only apparent. His full phantasy is to use his penis in order to get into the womb, to take possession of it, first as the baby in the womb, but with the eventual aim of robbing his mother and becoming her. It is a later genital elaboration of his original envy and rivalry with the mother, to which all other aims are subjected.

This contrasts with the position of another patient, who, when his analysis ended, was able to include homosexual components in his heterosexual life satisfactorily. He had lost his father when he was nine months old. His main complaint on coming to me was homosexuality in relation to children and young boys, and heterosexual impotence. It soon became apparent that one of his unconscious problems was passive homosexual wishes and fears in relation to older men, standing for his dead father; those wishes were never consciously experienced, as the dead father was also a threatening persecutor, whose assault he dreaded. In his pathology, he worked out his problem by projection and reversal, with himself in the rôle of the assaulting father. Towards the end of his analysis he lost his symptoms and became happily married. There was also a marked improvement in his personal relationships. Soon before the ending of his analysis, around Christmas time, and when he was hoping that his wife was pregnant, he had the following dream.

He dreamt that Father Christmas came down the chimney and gave him a parcel which he, the patient, was to give his wife for Christmas. In this dream, Father Christmas stands for myself, the analyst, who gave him the gift of potency and also for the dead and idealized father who gives him potency and babies to give to his wife. The descent down the chimney obviously represents anal intercourse. But here, in contrast to the previous patient, the homosexual gift that he wants from his father becomes the babies of his potency and creativity in relation to the woman. Further associations also made it clear that this combination of homo- and heterosexual elements expressed his wish to re-unite his father and mother symbolically in his own marriage.

It is impossible, of course, to cover the theme of the oedipus complex in one chapter. I have chosen to comment on some aspects only, which would help to illustrate the great importance of the early roots of the oedipal constellation, and the way it develops from a primitive oral relation to the genital situation described by Freud.

BIBLIOGRAPHY

PAULA HEIMANN: "A Contribution to the Re-evaluation of the Oedipus Complex," *New Directions in Psycho-analysis* (Chapter 2), Melanie Klein and others, *Int.J.Psycho-Anal.*, vol. 33 (1952).

MELANIE KLEIN: "Early Stages of the Oedipus Conflict," p. 202, *Contributions to Psycho-analysis*.

"The Oedipus Complex in the Light of Early Anxieties," p. 339, *Int.J.Psycho-Anal.* (1945).

CHAPTER TEN

POSTSCRIPT ON TECHNIQUE

IT IS VERY DIFFICULT to give an idea of psycho-analytical technique through description. In fact, the only way of becoming acquainted with another analyst's technique is through discussion of case material in supervision sessions, seminars, or study groups. The preceding chapters of this book are devoted to a discussion of theoretical concepts, using clinical material only as illustration. Some idea of the technique may be gleaned from certain reports of case-material in which I try to give the sequence of associations and interpretations, such as the child's material in Chapters 7 and 8 and some others. Other clinical illustrations, how-ever, can give a misleading impression in relation to tech-nique. For instance, I use dreams to illustrate certain basic mental mechanisms or structures, giving a possibly misleading impression that such material is interpreted directly in those terms, without establishing preconscious connections and links with the patient's actual external life, etc.

Questions are frequently asked about the extent to which Melanie Klein's discoveries and her concepts affect the psycho-analytic technique, and, conversely, to what extent this technique may influence the understanding of a patient's material. There is no doubt that there are some technical differences in dealing with the material which spring from Melanie Klein's theories, and that her technique in turn had an influence on the kind of material that became avail-able in and to the patient. It is a technical invention, namely the technique of child analysis, which gave Melanie

Klein access to the more primitive layers of the mind and led her to the discovery of the complex internal world in the child's mind and to the importance of the part played by projection and introjection in the building up of the child's internal mental structure and external relationships. This technique influenced theory.

Conversely, the new theoretical knowledge gained in that way was unavoidably reflected in her technique with adults. Such concepts as the paranoid–schizoid and depressive positions, naturally influence the way one sees the analytical material. For instance, in analysing an oedipal situation, an analyst familiar with these concepts will be particularly aware of the rôle projective identification may play in the perception of parental intercourse, of the nature of the internalized parental figures, and the way they are dealt with in the internal world.

It is Melanie Klein's contention that infantile neurosis is a way of binding and working through earlier anxieties of a psychotic nature. This view is nowadays widely held, probably by a majority of analysts, even though their views may differ on the precise mental content of the early infantile anxieties. This has far-reaching technical implications. For many analysts this is an indication for modifying the basic psycho-analytic method. In their view, the psycho-analytic method of interpretation is effective in relation to a whole-object triangular oedipal situation, but where it is essential to deal with earlier anxieties arising from the relationship between the baby and the breast, they contend, the psycho-analytic method is not in itself sufficient and the analyst has to provide an environmental factor to make up for the deficiency experienced in infancy. This necessitates in their view a departure from the neutral interpretative rôle of the analyst.

It is important for the understanding of Melanie Klein's technique to emphasize that this has never been her view. Here again theory and technique are intimately interlinked. In the early attempts at child-analysis, when controversies about technique were at their height, the classical view was that the small child's ego was too immature and the super-ego too weak to establish a psycho-analytic process, and that therefore the analyst should also adopt the rôle of a guiding figure to support the ego and strengthen the super-ego. Melanie Klein's view was that the small child's super-ego is harsher and more persecuting than in later stages of development and thus the rôle of the analyst is to lessen the severity of the super-ego by interpretation, allowing thereby the ego to develop more freely. In her view any departure from the analyst's neutral rôle interfered with this process. She had discovered that there was also sufficient ego development in any child who could speak, to establish a psycho-analytic relationship. She found this to be the case even in a psychotic non-speaking child ("The Importance of Symbol Formation in the Development of the Ego"). Her later discoveries and the conceptualization of developmental positions in no way altered this view. Indeed she and her followers consider that the deeper the analysis the more primitive the processes mobilized, the more essential it is to adhere rigorously to the basic psycho-analytic method. If the patient is to sort out what is external and what is internal, how far his view of the world is coloured by omnipotent phantasy, he can only do so if the analyst remains unaltered in his basic function by the patient's projections. This was expressed succinctly by a schizophrenic patient of mine. This patient was frequently late, and once when he came nearly at the end of his session he put great pressure on me to overstep the time, and in view of the precariousness of his situation I was very tempted to do so. But having interpreted to him the situation he had put me into, I terminated the session. The next day he expressed that it brought him tremendous relief and said "in my world you are the one person who knows the time. If you didn't know what time it was, then all would be lost."

Of course the rigorous adherence to the basic psycho-analytic method should not become rigidity. With certain patients it may sometimes be necessary to start with seven times a week; with some psychotics, as with small children, provision may have to be made for their being brought and fetched from the sessions, etc. But once the setting has been established it should not be subject to control by the patient's illness. The patient projects onto the analyst his internal figures and also parts of his own ego. The iller the patient the more unconsciously determined he is to get the analyst to act out for him those projections. Any such acting-out on the part of the analyst is in effect a confirmation of the patient's omnipotence and also an impoverishment of his personality through the losses incurred by such projections. It is the analyst's acceptance and understanding of these projections, without acting them out, and the gradual conveying back to the patient of the psychic content, that gives to the patient the basic security of being contained in the psycho-analytic situation.

I want to emphasize that the basic psycho-analytical setting, attitude and methodology, is not only unaltered by our theoretical views but rather strengthened by them. For instance, the understanding of how projective identification works makes it more evident why it is essential for the analyst not to step out of his rôle. On the other hand, details of technique, the actual handling of the material, are unavoidably influenced by one's views on the psychodynamics involved. For instance, following the processes of projection and introjection in the building up of the internal world leads to a more consistent intervention by interpretation. The analyst interprets more what the patient attributes to him and how he internalizes him. He may follow the effect of the interpretation on the patient's further material and he is generally more concerned with the to-and-fro of the interchange than is the case in the purely classical technique. The emphasis on transference is also greater. This again is linked with theoretical views. As I tried to show in my chapter on phantasy, the Kleinian view is that the relation to the external world, and indeed interest in the external world, springs from externalization and symbolization of unconscious phantasy. Since the analyst comes to stand for the internal figures, all the material that the patient brings contains a dynamic element of transference. When I say "transference interpretation" I do not mean by this a here-and-now interpretation. A full transference interpretation should include the current external relationship in the patient's life, the patient's relationship to the analyst, and the relation between these and the relationships with the parents in the past. It should also aim at establishing a link between the internal figures and the external ones. Of course such an interpretation would have to be long and is seldom made fully, but for a transference interpretation to be complete at some point or other those elements should be brought together.

Our understanding of the rôle of unconscious phantasy in mental structure leads therefore to a stronger emphasis on transference. It also leads to a different way of interpreting mental mechanisms. The question is often asked, "What is the difference between interpreting a projection and interpreting projective identification?" In interpreting projection one indicates to the patient that he is attributing to another person a characteristic which is in fact his own. In interpreting projective identification one tries to interpret the detail of the phantasy. I give an example of this kind of interpretation in the child's material of the fox in Chapter 3. One aims at making the patient aware of the motives of the projective phantasy, and its effects on the perception of the object and of the self. For instance, one can show a patient how the projection of his own aggressive sexuality into the parental intercourse, gives rise both to the perception of his parents as cruel and sexually dangerous, and also to the perception of himself as devoid of aggression and sex. It is very important in interpreting projective identification not to "shove back" into the patient automatically what he had projected. Ad hoc interpretations of the kind "You put your anger into me" or "your distrust into me" without further elaboration, are experienced by the patient as persecutory pushing back what had been projected. One has to interpret always in the context of the whole relationship, taking into account the patient's motives, anxieties and the aim of the projections. I had a patient who before her analysis with me had had several analytic treatments which had failed because of her obstinate silence. To begin with, her silence was linked with projective identification, but as it proceeded, the meaning of it kept changing. At first I interpreted it primarily as a communication: I interpreted to her that she wanted to make me experience what it felt like to be cut off and unable to communicate. Later on, when she was on the threshold of the depressive position, I interpreted that she wanted to make me feel what it is like to have a lifeless internal object (herself on the couch) and to feel both guilty about it and helpless in bringing it to life. Later on, as the patient's distress and her need to project in order to communicate, had lessened a great deal, when she was silent the silence was much more aggressive. Now I could interpret the projection into me of feelings of failure and inadequacy, the motives being two-fold: she partly wanted to get rid of such feelings from within herself and partly wanted to project them into me out of revenge, spite and envy. In any of these situations, when she was silent a vicious circle was established, in which her projection into me of painful feelings led to an anxiety that I would push it back into her and therefore the silence would acquire also a defensive aspect—not speaking in order not to let me penetrate her by interpretations; and this in turn had to be interpreted.

This of course raises the question of how much one interprets, particularly with a silent patient. Here the style of every analyst will be different, and he will be guided by the total situation. In the patient I described, to begin with I used to interpret a fair amount, as it was quite clear she could not speak until I established contact with her by understanding her projective identification, and enabled her to tolerate the reintegration of the active parts of herself so that she could speak. But later on in the treatment, particularly when the silence was of an aggressive kind, or defensive against a context that seemed near consciousness, I used to be silent for long stretches. The patient herself was aware of the reason for the change in my dealing with her silence, because, one day, after having complained bitterly that in the past I used to interpret her silence but now was more often silent, she added "but I suppose then you had no choice."

One cannot divorce considerations of technique from views on the dynamic factors in the analytical process and from the therapeutic aim. When Freud discovered the dynamic unconscious processes and the defence mechanism of repression, the aim of the psycho-analytic technique was to lift repressions and render the unconscious conscious— "where id was there ego shall be." Has this basic aim been altered by later discoveries? Basically the therapeutic aim has remained the same—to free the ego and enable it to grow and mature and establish satisfactory object relations. Now, however, we know more about the complex structure of internal objects and about the growth of the ego, not only as a maturational process but also as promoted or hindered by the relationship it has with its internal objects. We know something about the distortions in ego-development due to anxiety-ridden internal object relations and defensive processes directly affecting the wholeness of the ego, such as, for instance, splitting, fragmentation, pathological projective identification. The analysis of these processes restores the ego's capacity for a more correct perception of objects and enables it to achieve a more constructive object relationship which in turn can play its part in growth.

The problem is often raised at analytical symposia whether the mutuative factors in psycho-analysis are more related to insight or to a corrective object relationship. It seems to me that these two factors are inseparable because it is only in the security of the analytical relationship with the analyst as a partner who does not project or react but aims at understanding, that true insight can develop. On the other hand, it is only through insight into one's own psyche that a better object relationship can be established in relation to both internal and external reality. The search for psychic realities remains the prime object of the psycho-analytic process.

BIBLIOGRAPHY

Adult Technique
HANNA SEGAL: "Melanie Klein's technique" in *Psychoanalytic Techniques*, ed. Wolman (New York: Basic Books, 1967).

Child Technique
MELANIE KLEIN: *Psycho-Analysis of Children* (London: Hogarth, 1932).
"Richard" in *Narrative of a Child Analysis* (London: Hogarth, 1961).
DONALD MELTZER: *The Psychoanalytical Process* (London: Heinemann Medical, 1967).
HANNA SEGAL: "Melanie Klein's technique" in *Handbook of child psychoanalysis*, ed. Wolman (New York: Van Nostrand Reinhold Company, 1967).

GLOSSARY

This glossary does not aim at being comprehensive. It contains terms which students most frequently asked to have elucidated. Some of them were introduced by Melanie Klein or her co-workers, others are in common analytic usage but are given as well because of the specific way in which they are used in Melanie Klein's work.

ANXIETY: is considered to be the ego's response to the operation of the death instinct. When the death instinct is deflected it takes two major forms:

Paranoid Anxiety is due to the projection of the death instinct into an object or objects which are then experienced as persecutors. The anxiety is lest these persecutors should annihilate the ego and the ideal object. It originates in the paranoid–schizoid position.

Depressive Anxiety is the anxiety lest one's own aggression should annihilate or has annihilated one's good object. It is experienced on behalf of the object and on behalf of the ego, which feels threatened in identification with the object. It originates in the depressive position, when the object is perceived as a whole object and the infant experiences his own ambivalence.

Castration Anxiety is mainly of a paranoid type originating in the child's projection of his own aggression, but it may contain depressive elements as well; for instance, the anxiety of losing one's penis as an organ of reparation.

BIZARRE OBJECTS: are the outcome of pathological projective identifications in which the object is perceived as split into minute fragments, each containing a projected part of the self. These bizarre objects are experienced as being charged with great hostility.

COMBINED PARENTS: a phantasy figure of parents combined in intercourse. It originates when the father is not fully differentiated from the mother and his penis is felt as part of mother's body. When oedipal anxieties are aroused this phantasy is reactivated regressively as a means of denial of the parental intercourse. It is usually experienced as a terrifying figure.

DEPRESSIVE POSITION: is ushered in when the infant recognizes his mother as a whole object. It is a constellation of object relations and anxieties characterized by the infant's experience of attacking an ambivalently loved mother and losing her as an external and internal object. This experience gives rise to pain, guilt and feelings of loss.

DEPRESSION: is a state of mind in which painful feelings of the depressive position are partly or fully experienced. It may be a normal reaction to experiences of loss or pathological in a neurotic or psychotic way.

EARLY ENVY: is experienced by the infant mainly in relation to the feeding breast. It is possibly the earliest external manifestation of the death instinct as it attacks what is felt to be the source of life.

Excessive early envy is an important factor in psychopathology.

EARLY OEDIPUS COMPLEX: is the oedipal relation experienced by the infant as from the beginning of the depressive position. It is experienced in pre-genital terms before genitality is reached.

GUILT: is the painful realization of having damaged one's loved object or objects. It originates in the depressive position when ambivalence is experienced towards the parents perceived as whole objects. The ambivalently loved parents introjected in the depressive position form the core of the super-ego.

IDEALIZATION: is a schizoid mechanism, connected with splitting and denial. The unwanted characteristics of an object are denied and the infant's own libido is projected into the object. Though pertaining primarily to the paranoid–schizoid position, idealization can be used a part of the manic defences against depressive anxieties.

IDENTIFICATION: is considered always to be an outcome of introjective or projective processes.

Introjective identification is the result when the object is introjected into the ego which then identifies with some or all of its characteristics.

Projective identification is the result of the projection of parts of the self into an object. It may result in the object being perceived as having acquired the characteristics of the projected part of the self but it can also result in the self becoming identified with the object of its projection.

Pathological projective identification is a result of minute disintegration of the self or parts of the self which are then projected into the object and disintegrated; it results in the creation of "bizarre objects."

INTERNAL OBJECTS: are objects introjected into the ego.

INTERNAL WORLD: is the result of the operation of unconscious phantasy, in which objects are introjected and a complex internal world is built up within the ego, in which the internal objects are felt to be in a dynamic relationship to one another and to the ego.

MANIC DEFENCES: are evolved in the depressive position as a defence against the experience of depressive anxiety, guilt and loss. They are based on an omnipotent denial of psychic reality and object relations are characterized by triumph, control and contempt.

PARANOID–SCHIZOID POSITION: is tne earliest phase of development. It is characterized by the relation to part objects, the prevalence of splitting in the ego and in the object and paranoid anxiety.

PART OBJECTS: are objects characteristic of the paranoid–schizoid position. The first part object experienced by the infant is the breast. Soon other part objects are experienced—first of all the penis.

Ideal object—breast or penis, is experienced by the infant in the paranoid–schizoid position as a result of splitting and denial of persecution. All the infant's good experiences, real and phantasied, are attributed to this ideal object which he longs to possess and identify with.

Bad (or Persecuting) Object is experienced as a result of the splitting in the paranoid–schizoid position. Into it is projected all the infant's hostility and all bad experiences are attributed to its activities.

Good object: the good part-object is usually applied to the breast or penis as it is experienced in the depressive position in relationship to good experiences. It is felt as a source of life, love and goodness, but it is not ideal. Its bad qualities are recognized and it may be experienced as frustrating in contrast to the ideal object; it is felt to be vulnerable to attacks, and therefore it is often experienced as damaged or destroyed. The good breast and the good penis are felt as belonging respectively to the good mother and the good father, but they may be experienced before the whole-object relationship is fully established.

PERSECUTORS: are objects into whom part of the death instinct has been projected. They give rise to paranoid anxiety.

PSYCHIC REALITY: The experience of psychic reality is the experience of one's internal world, including the experience of impulses and the internal objects.

REALITY SENSE: is the capacity to experience psychic reality as such and to differentiate it from external reality. It involves the simultaneous experience and correlation of the internal and external worlds.

REPARATION: is an ego activity directed at restoring a loved injured object. It arises in the depressive position as a reaction to depressive anxieties and guilt. Reparation may be used as part of the system of manic defences, in which case it acquires the manic characteristics of denial, control and contempt.

SPLITTING: can involve the ego and the object. The earliest splitting is between the good and the bad self and the good and the bad object. The deflection of the death instinct involves a splitting of the part felt to contain the destructive impulses from the part felt to contain the libido.

WHOLE OBJECTS: describes the perception of another person as a person. The perception of the mother as a whole object characterizes the depressive position. The whole object contrasts both with the part-object and with objects split into ideal and persecutory parts. Ambivalence and guilt are experienced in relation to whole-objects.

BIBLIOGRAPHY OF MELANIE KLEIN

(in order of first publication in English)

(1921) "The development of a child" *Int.J.Psycho-Anal.*, *4*; and in *Contributions*.*

(1923) "The role of the school in the libidinal development of the child" *Int.J.Psycho-Anal.*, *5*; and in *Contributions*.*

(1926) "Infant analysis" *Int.J.Psycho-Anal.*, *7*; and in *Contributions*.*

(1926) "The psychological principles of infant analysis" *Int.J.Psycho-Anal.*, *8*; and in *Contributions*.*

(1927) Contribution to "Symposium on Child Analysis" *Int.J.Psycho-Anal.*, *8*; and in *Contributions*.*

(1927) "Criminal tendencies in normal children" *Brit.J. med.Psycho.*, *7*; and in *Contributions*.*

(1928) "Early stages of the Oedipus complex" *Int.J. Psycho-Anal.*, *9*; and in *Contributions*.*

(1928) "Notes on 'A Dream of Forensic Interest' by D. Bryan" *Int.J.Psycho-Anal.*, *9*.

(1929) "Personification in the play of children" *Int.J. Psycho-Anal.*, *10*; and in *Contributions*.*

(1929) "Infantile anxiety situations reflected in a work of art and in the creative impulse" *Int.J.Psycho-Anal.*, *10*; and in *Contributions*.*

(1930) "The importance of symbol-formation in the development of the ego" *Int.J.Psycho-Anal.*, *11*; and in *Contributions*.*

(1930) "The psychotherapy of the psychoses" *Brit.J. med.Psychol.*, *10*; and in *Contributions*.*

(1931) "A contribution to the theory of intellectual inhibition" *Int.J.Psycho-Anal.*, *12*; and in *Contributions*.*

* *Contributions to Psycho-Analysis, 1921-45* (London: Hogarth, 1948).

(1932) *The Psycho-Analysis of Children* (London: Hogarth).

(1933) "The early development of conscience in the child" in *Psychoanalysis Today* ed. Lorand (New York: Covici-Friede); and in *Contributions*.*

(1934) "On criminality" *Brit.J.med.Psychol.*, *14*; and in *Contributions*.*

(1935) "A contribution to the psychogenesis of manic-depressive states" *Int.J.Psycho-Anal.*, *16*; and in *Contributions*.*

(1936) "Weaning" in *On the Bringing up of Children* ed. Rickman (London: Routledge).

(1937) "Love, guilt and reparation" in *Love, Hate and Reparation*, with J. Riviere (London: Hogarth).

(1940) "Mourning and its relation to manic-depressive states" *Int.J.Psycho-Anal.*, *21*; and in *Contributions*.*

(1942) "Some psychological considerations" contributed to *Science and Ethics* ed. Waddington (London: Allen & Unwin).

(1945) "The Oedipus complex in the light of early anxieties" *Int.J.Psycho-Anal.*, *26*; and in *Contributions*.*

(1946) "Notes on some schizoid mechanisms" *Int.J. Psycho-Anal.*, *27*; and in *Developments in Psycho-Analysis* (1952).

(1948) "A contribution to the psychogenesis of tics" in *Contributions*.*

(1948) *Contributions to Psycho-Analysis, 1921–45* (London: Hogarth).

(1948) "A contribution to the theory of anxiety and guilt" *Int.J.Psycho-Anal.*, *29*; and in *Developments in Psycho-Analysis* (1952).

(1950) "On the criteria for the termination of a psycho-analysis" *Int.J.Psycho-Anal.*, *31*.

(1952) "The origins of transference" *Int.J.Psycho-Anal.*, *33*.

(1952) "Some theoretical conclusions regarding the emotional life of the infant" in *Developments in Psycho-Analysis* (1952).

(1952) "On observing the behaviour of young infants" in *Developments in Psycho-Analysis* (1952).

* *Contributions to Psycho-Analysis, 1921–45* (London: Hogarth, 1948).

(1952) *Developments in Psycho-Analysis* ed. J. Riviere (London: Hogarth).

(1952) "The mutual influences in the development of ego and id" *Psycho-Anal. Study Child*, 7.

(1955) "The psycho-analytic play technique: its history and significance" in *New Directions in Psycho-Analysis* (1955).

(1955) "On identification" in *New Directions in Psycho-Analysis* (1955).

(1955) *New Directions in Psycho-Analysis*, with P. Heimann, R. Money-Kyrle, *et al.* (London: Tavistock; New York: Basic Books).

(1956) "The psychoanalytic play technique" *Amer.J. Orthopsychiat.*, 25.

(1957) *Envy and Gratitude* (London: Tavistock; New York: Basic Books).

(1958) "The development of mental functioning" *Int.J. Psycho-Anal.*, 39.

(1959) "Our adult world and its roots in infancy" *Hum. Relations*, 12; and in *Our Adult World and Other Essays* (1963).

(1961) *Narrative of a Child Analysis* (London: Hogarth; New York: Basic Books).

(1963) "On identification" in *Our Adult World and Other Essays* (1963).

(1963) "On the sense of loneliness" (1960) in *Our Adult World and Other Essays* (1963).

(1963) "Some reflections on 'The Oresteia'" (posthumous) in *Our Adult World and Other Essays* (1963).

(1963) *Our Adult World and Other Essays* (London: Heinemann; New York: Basic Books).

SOME SIGNIFICANT DISCUSSIONS OF
MELANIE KLEIN'S WORK

BRIERLEY, Marjorie. 1951: "Problems connected with the Work of Melanie Klein." Chapter III in *Trends in Psycho-Analysis* (London: Hogarth).

GLOVER, Edward. 1933: Review of *The Psycho-Analysis of Children* by Melanie Klein. *Int.J.Psycho-Anal.*, *14*, pp. 119–29.

GUNTRIP, Harry. 1961: "The Psychodynamic Theory of Melanie Klein" and "Melanie Klein: Theory of Early Development and 'Psychotic' Positions." Chapters 11 and 12 in *Personality Structure and Human Interaction* (London: Hogarth).

JOFFE, W. G. 1969: "A Critical Review of the Status of the Envy Concept." *Int.J.Psycho-Anal.*, *50*, pp. 533–45.

MONEY-KYRLE, Roger. 1966: "British Schools of Psycho-analysis: Melanie Klein and Kleinian Psychoanalytic Theory" in *American Handbook of Psychiatry*, vol. 3, edited by Silvano Arieti (New York: Basic Books).

PAYNE, S. M. 1946: "Notes on Developments in the Theory and Practice of Psycho-Analytical Technique." *Int.J.Psycho-Anal.*, *27*, pp. 12–19.

RICKMAN, John. 1950: "The Development of Psychological Medicine" in *Selected Contributions to Psycho-Analysis* (London: Hogarth, 1957).

SCOTT, W. Clifford M. 1949: "Psychoanalysis: The Kleinian View." *British Medical Bulletin*, Vol. 6, No. 1–2, pp. 31–35.

SEGAL, Hanna. 1967: "Melanie Klein's Technique" in *Psycho-analytic Techniques*, edited by Benjamin B. Wolman (New York: Basic Books).

SMIRNOFF, Victor. 1966: "Phantasmes inconscients et Consti-tution de l'objet dans les conceptions de Melanie Klein" and "Les conceptions de Melanie Klein," Chapter V, Part III, and Chapter VI, Part III, in *La Psychanalyse de l'enfant* (Paris: Presses Universitaires de France).

WINNICOTT, D. W.   1935: "The Manic Defence" in *Collected Papers* (London: Tavistock Publications, 1958).

1955: "The Depressive Position in Normal Emotional Development" in *Collected Papers* (London: Tavistock Publications, 1958).

1958: "Psycho-Analysis and the Sense of Guilt" in *The Maturational Processes and the Facilitating Environment* (London: Hogarth, 1965).

1959: Review of *Envy and Gratitude* by Melanie Klein in *Case Conference* 5.

1962: "A Personal View of the Kleinian Contribution" in *The Maturational Processes*, 1965.

ZETZEL, Elizabeth R.   1953: "The Depressive Position" in *The Capacity for Emotional Growth* (London: Hogarth, 1970).

1956: "Concept and Content in Psychoanalytic Theory" in *ibid.*

INDEX

Aggression,
  acknowledgement of in reparation,
    101
  and attack on words, 97
  and death instinct, 25
  expressed and responsibility taken
    for, 33
  Klein's reevaluation of, 9
  and libido, 3
Aggressive instincts, projected into
  father, 21
Ambition, immoderate, in envious
  patient, 43
Ambivalence,
  acute in early oedipal situation
    109
  and depressive experience, 83
  and loved object in depressive
    position, 69 *et seq.*
  prevalent in depressive position, ix
Anal gratifications projected by
  infant, 103
Analyst,
  as acceptor of projections, 120
  attacked as mother in oedipal
    situation, 94
  attacked as successful enviously
    potent father, 42
  and husband, representing parents
    in oedipal situation, 106
  as departing mother, 96
  as depriving, destroyed, retaliating
    breast, 77
  as depriving mother, 85
  as displaced, pregnant mother, 114
  as envied, attacked mother, 43
  as exhausted and impoverished, 87
  as external, devalued father, 88
  as good and bad breast splits in two,
    17
  as ideal, depleting object, 59
  as ill child in reversal situation,
    77
  as internal figures, 120
  as internalized father, 45

Analyst—*cont.*
  as invulnerable ideal breast, 61
  as omnipotently controlled agent in
    manic reparation, 98
  as part-object (magical penis), 98
  as realistic, helpful analyst, 101
  as restoring father, 100
  as split parental figure, 32
  as whole person, 101
  competed for as mother-figure,
    48
  containing eggs and babies, 29
  dangerous animal, 29
  endowed with magic powers, 99
  holiday of, representing parental
    intercourse and pregnancy, 96
  identified with bad introjected
    penis, 30
  identified with envied mother, 77
  "in the gutter" (destroyed by
    omnipotent envy), 46, 47
  "on a pedestal" (inside envious
    patient), 44 *et seq.*
  split into ideal and worthless
    figures, 18, 19
Analyst's written work, representing
  babies, 108
  combined masculine potency and
    female fertility, 108
Annihilation, fear of, 26
Anti-semitism, unconscious, 94
Anxiety,
  see also Castration fears, Depressive
    anxiety, Paranoid anxiety,
    Persecutory anxiety
  leading to regression, 110, 112

Bad object,
  see also Persecutory objects
  attempts to keep out, 26
  breast containing deflected death
    instinct, 25
  destroyed parental couple, 91
  internal dead father, 102
  phantasied torn breast, 13, 14